The Gen X Series

OLYMPIAD WORKBOOK

NATIONAL SCIENCE OLYMPIAD

01 Learning Objectives

02 Multiple Choice Questions

03 HOTS (Achievers Section)

04 Model Test Paper

05 Answer Keys and Solutions

06 OMR Answer Sheet

V&S PUBLISHERS

Published by:

F-2/16, Ansari road, Daryaganj, New Delhi-110002
☎ 23240026, 23240027 • *Fax:* 011-23240028
info@vspublishers.com • www.vspublishers.com

Online Brandstore: amazon.in/vspublishers

Regional Office : Hyderabad
5-1-707/1, Brij Bhawan (Beside Central Bank of India Lane)
Bank Street, Koti, Hyderabad - 500 095
☎ 040-24737290
vspublishershyd@gmail.com

Follow us on:   

BUY OUR BOOKS FROM: AMAZON FLIPKART

New Edition

DISCLAIMER

While every attempt has been made to provide accurate and timely information in this book, neither the author nor the publisher assumes any responsibility for errors, unintended omissions or commissions detected therein. The author and publisher makes no representation or warranty with respect to the comprehensiveness or completeness of the contents provided.

All matters included have been simplified under professional guidance for general information only, without any warranty for applicability on an individual. Any mention of an organization or a website in the book, by way of citation or as a source of additional information, doesn't imply the endorsement of the content either by the author or the publisher. It is possible that websites cited may have changed or removed between the time of editing and publishing the book.

Results from using the expert opinion in this book will be totally dependent on individual circumstances and factors beyond the control of the author and the publisher.

It makes sense to elicit advice from well informed sources before implementing the ideas given in the book. The reader assumes full responsibility for the consequences arising out from reading this book.

For proper guidance, it is advisable to read the book under the watchful eyes of parents/guardian. The buyer of this book assumes all responsibility for the use of given materials and information.

Printed at : Param Offsetters, Okhla, New Delhi–110020

PUBLISHER'S NOTE

V&S Publishers has carved a significant niche in the publishing industry over the last decade, having successfully published more than 1000 titles across 9 languages spanning over 50 subject categories. Being known for the quality of content, we have built a reputation of excellence and reliability. We have consistently delivered **"Value & Substance"** to our readers, through a wide range of titles across a variety of genres covering school books, fiction and non-fiction that caters to different people from every section of the society.

The **Olympiad Guidebooks for classes 1-10** across all subjects, launched almost a decade ago, under the **GEN X Imprint**, became a go-to-source for the school students in no time, owing to their invaluable and substantive content written in a guidebook pattern,.

Having successfully sold a million copies of the same and in response to demand by both students as well as shopkeepers nationwide; we now present before you our newly launched **Olympiad Workbook Series**, designed for **classes 1-10 across 4 subjects**.

The workbooks are meticulously curated by a team of experienced educators, researchers and subject matter experts, edited by professionals and peer reviewed by teachers. The team has poured its efforts and expertise into creating a crisp and concise workbook which will help and guide the students to the path of success in Olympiad exams. The **MCQs** identified will not only help in scoring top marks in Olympiads but also inculcate a sense of deeper understanding of the subject, by way of solving **HOTS** and referring to complete solutions at the end of the book.

Here we present our new release– **OLYMPIAD WORKBOOK (NSO) CLASS-5** having following features:

- ☞ Based on the latest syllabi
- ☞ MCQs with comprehensive coverage of topics
- ☞ HOTS Questions liberally included
- ☞ A dedicated chapter on logical reasoning
- ☞ Model test paper for thorough practice
- ☞ Sample OMR sheet for real time simulation

We have made sure through our best efforts, that this workbook strictly follows the latest syllabi and patterns of the Olympiad Examination.

As **V&S Publishers** continuously strive to enhance the readability and maintain the credibility of our academic publications, we seek the support of our valuable readers in influencing and enriching the lives of future generations of students.

P.S. While every care has been taken to ensure the correctness of the content, if you come across any error, howsoever minor, do not hesitate to discuss with teachers while pointing that out to us in no uncertain terms.

We wish you all the best for your exams!

DISTINCTIVE FEATURES

WHY OLYMPIADS?

Olympiads are just like competitive exams; conducted by various bodies at national and international levels. The aim is to experience a competitive examination at the school level and also to help students to discover their interest across subjects like English, Mathematics, Science and General Knowledge.

COMPLEMENTS SCHOOL SYLLABI

The syllabi across all Olympiad examination closely follow the pattern of academic books. Hence, they not only provide a competitive examination experience, but also help to revise topics for school examinations as well, while strengthening conceptual precision.

01

Learning Objectives

They list the whole chapter as subtopics, helping the teachers to guide children in a step-by-step manner.

02

Multiple Choice Questions

MCQs act as an excellent learning aid, helping you to understand and work on your mistakes.

03

HOTS (Achievers Section)

The High Order Thinking Questions aim to help the student to solve Application-based questions and gain practical understanding of the subject.

Model Test Paper

Model test paper are provided at the end of each book, which help the student to test the knowledge which they have gained after thorough reading of all chapters.

04

Answer Key

Detailed Answer Key along with explanations aid the pupil to indentify, understand the mistakes they make during the course of Olympiad preparation.

05

WHY V&S OLYMPIADS?

We at V&S Publishers aim to build an avid-reading student audience. Hence, our resolve is to follow an innovative pedagogic pattern which would help students to navigate through the book with utmost ease and comfort. Crisp theory, practical examples and illustrations keep our book interactive and comprehensive.

ANALYTICAL & LOGICAL REASONING

Practicing analytical ability questions, not only helps in developing intellectual ability but also plays a vital role in building critical thinking ability which helps an individual to think about a question or a crisis like situation in day to day life; from all aspects and directions.

CONTENTS

ANIMALS

LEARNING OBJECTIVES

- ➤ Animals and its two groups: vertebrates and invertebrates
- ➤ Relationship between habits and habitat
- ➤ Adaptations of animal

MULTIPLE CHOICE QUESTIONS

Direction: Select the correct option.

1. A habitat is __________.
   (A) An animal's immediate natural surroundings which contains an arrangement of food, water, shelter or cover, and space that meets the animal's needs.
   (B) A place containing an arrangement of food, water, shelter or cover, and space.
   (C) An animal's immediate natural surroundings or environment.
   (D) The surroundings in which a plant or an animal grows and lives which suits their needs.

2. Ecosystem can be defined as __________.
   (A) An interacting system of living organisms and non-living parts of the environment.
   (B) The place where these interactions (stated in point A) take place.
   (C) An interactive system of living organisms and non-living parts of the environment where these interactions take place.
   (D) A network of interconnected food chains.

3. Which category of animals makes up 90 per cent of the animal world?
   (A) Mammals
   (B) Vertebrates
   (C) Soft-bodied animals
   (D) Invertebrates

4. Which group of animals have been on earth the longest?
   (A) Birds (B) Mammals
   (C) Whales (D) Fish

5. Like water beetles, which other animal breathes oxygen from the air, renewing its supply of air on the surface?
   (A) Back swimmer (B) Water striders
   (C) Water flea (D) Water strider

6. Which of the following have hearing organs on their front legs?
   (A) Squirrel (B) Viper
   (C) Rabbit (D) Bush cricket

7. Who am I?
   I swim in swamps, I bloat my cheeks,
   I dive in dams and croak in creeks.
   (A) Emu
   (B) Water Holding Frog
   (C) Green and Golden Bell Frog
   (D) Penguins

8. Which of the following is a correct match with the given headings?

	Can fly	**Cannot fly**
(A)	Emu	Crow
(B)	Sparrow	Pigeon
(C)	Kiwi	Ostrich
(D)	Parrot	Penguin

9. Which of these animals camouflage with its surrounding?

(A) (B)

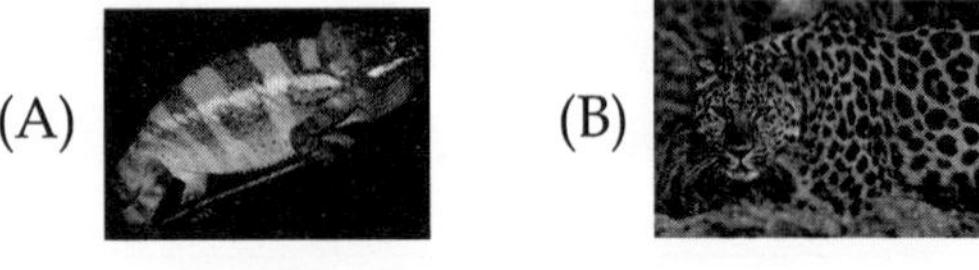

(C)

(D) All of these

10. Choose the correct option to answer the sentence below:

Animals return water to the environment by__________

(i) Perspiring (ii) Drinking
(iii) Urinating (iv) Breathing

(A) (i), (iii) and (iv)
(B) (i) and (ii)
(C) (i) and (iii)
(D) (iii) and (iv)

11. Study the given Venn diagram carefully. Which alphabet represents fish?

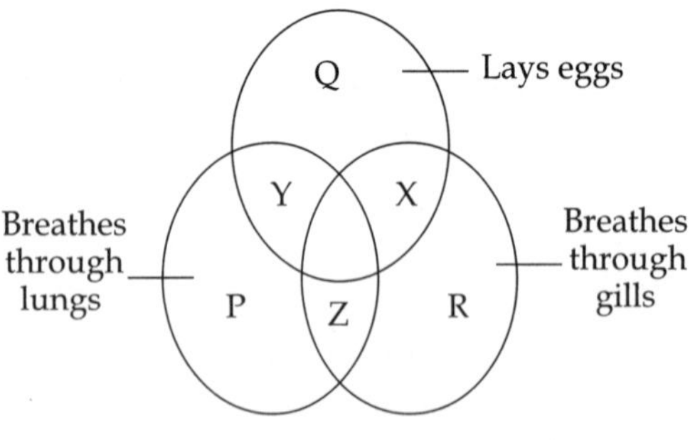

(A) Y (B) X
(C) Z (D) P

12. In the following list, one organism does not correlate because it eats different types of food than the other organisms in the list. Cross off the organism that does not correlate.

	Carnivore	**Producer**
(A)	Green crab	Phytoplankton
(B)	Minnow	Seaweed
(C)	Sea bass	Marsh grass
(D)	Algae	Ribbed mussel

13. Which invertebrate is the most advanced?

(A) Octopus (B) Spider
(C) Jellyfish (D) Barnacles

14. Which of the following statements about fishes is not true?

(A) All fish have gills.
(B) All fish live in water.
(C) All fish use fins for balance.
(D) All fish are warm blooded.

15. What does a jellyfish use to catch food?

(A) Sponges (B) Limbs
(C) Stinging cells (D) Muscles

16. Look at the Venn diagram and choose the correct option from the following:

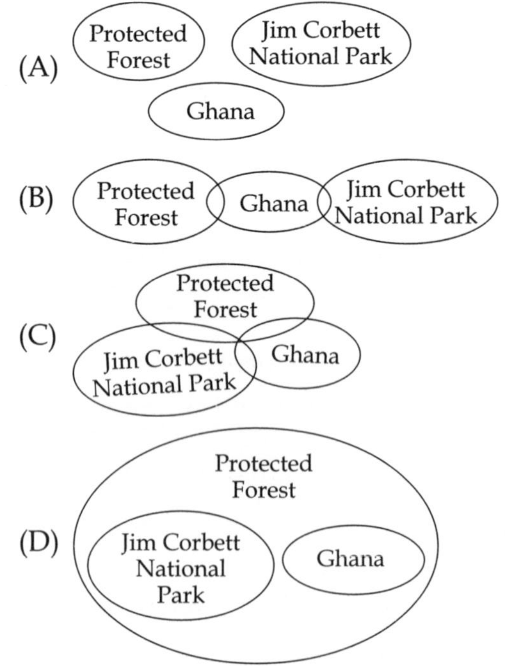

17. Cranes and herons have long legs with spread-out toes. They can be categorized as __________.
(A) Flying birds
(B) Water birds
(C) Wading birds
(D) Perching birds

18. In the given figure of the lifecycle of a butterfly, what does stage 3 represent?

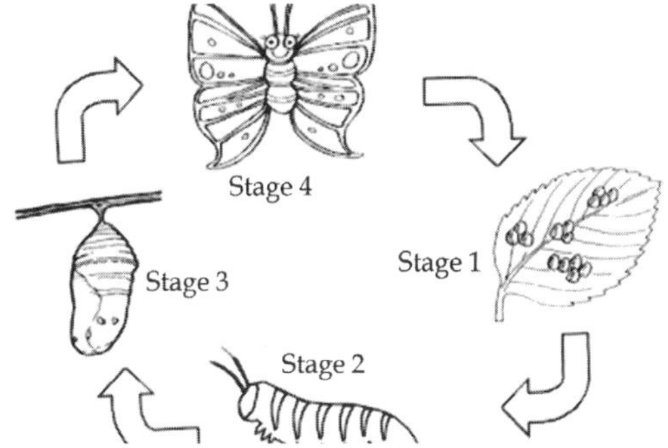

(A) Caterpillar (B) Pupa
(C) Nymph (D) Adult

19. Animals migrate __________.
(A) To reach their breeding groups
(B) To escape harsh weather
(C) To search for food
(D) All of these

20. Which of the following statements is true?
(A) The mass movement of animals from one place to another is known as hibernation.
(B) Gills are special organs with which all mammals breathe.
(C) Emu is a flightless bird.
(D) Mammals like ants and cockroaches crawl on their legs.

21. Drop some jaggery on the ground and observe it for a while. Now look at the following statements and mark the ones that are true.
(A) In the beginning, only one ant comes near the jaggery.
(B) In the beginning, a group of ants come near the jaggery.
(C) In the beginning, only one ant comes near the jaggery and as the ants move, they leave a smell on the ground.
(D) As the ants move, they produce light.

22. I can spot my prey from miles away: __________.
(A) Ant
(B) Eagle
(C) Rat
(D) Leopard

23. Mosquitoes can find you by the __________.
(A) Sound of your body
(B) Smell of your body
(C) Shadow of your body
(D) All of these

24. The animal shown in the picture below warns other animals of dangers such as the arrival of a tiger or leopard, by:

(A) Producing some chemicals
(B) Making a special warning call
(C) Dancing
(D) None of these

25. It looks like a bear but is not. It spends almost 17 hours a day sleeping while hanging upside down on a tree branch. It lives for about 40 years and in that time moves around only eight trees. Guess which animal am I.

The animal referred to in the above paragraph is a __________.
(A) Monkey (B) Sloth
(C) Bat (D) Gibbon

HOTS (ACHIEVERS SECTION)

26. Mountain lions give birth to their young ones in the spring. How does this reproductive adaptation increase the young mountain lions' survival?
    (A) Spring time temperature make predators hibernate.
    (B) More food is available to young ones during spring.
    (C) There is less competition for warmth in spring.
    (D) Predators only eat plants during spring.

27. The organisms given below are similar as they all

    (A) crawl.
    (B) fly.
    (C) eat insects.
    (D) take care of their young ones.

28. Study the table given below. Which of these is incorrectly matched?

	Animal	Outer covering
(A)	Polar bear	Fur
(B)	Leopard	Feather
(C)	Turtle	Shell
(D)	Snake	Scales

29. Which of the following animals breathe through gills?

A.  B. 

C.  D. 

    (A) D only
    (B) Only A and C
    (C) Only B and C
    (D) Only A, B and C

30. What is the adaptation by which a grasshopper protects itself from being eaten by its predator?
    (A) It tastes bad.
    (B) It can hop away quickly.
    (C) It can camouflage itself in the grass.
    (D) It has a poisonous sting.

Darken Your Choice with HB Pencil

1.	Ⓐ Ⓑ Ⓒ Ⓓ	7.	Ⓐ Ⓑ Ⓒ Ⓓ	13.	Ⓐ Ⓑ Ⓒ Ⓓ	19	Ⓐ Ⓑ Ⓒ Ⓓ	25.	Ⓐ Ⓑ Ⓒ Ⓓ
2.	Ⓐ Ⓑ Ⓒ Ⓓ	8.	Ⓐ Ⓑ Ⓒ Ⓓ	14.	Ⓐ Ⓑ Ⓒ Ⓓ	20.	Ⓐ Ⓑ Ⓒ Ⓓ	26.	Ⓐ Ⓑ Ⓒ Ⓓ
3.	Ⓐ Ⓑ Ⓒ Ⓓ	9.	Ⓐ Ⓑ Ⓒ Ⓓ	15.	Ⓐ Ⓑ Ⓒ Ⓓ	21.	Ⓐ Ⓑ Ⓒ Ⓓ	27.	Ⓐ Ⓑ Ⓒ Ⓓ
4.	Ⓐ Ⓑ Ⓒ Ⓓ	10.	Ⓐ Ⓑ Ⓒ Ⓓ	16.	Ⓐ Ⓑ Ⓒ Ⓓ	22.	Ⓐ Ⓑ Ⓒ Ⓓ	28.	Ⓐ Ⓑ Ⓒ Ⓓ
5.	Ⓐ Ⓑ Ⓒ Ⓓ	11.	Ⓐ Ⓑ Ⓒ Ⓓ	17.	Ⓐ Ⓑ Ⓒ Ⓓ	23.	Ⓐ Ⓑ Ⓒ Ⓓ	29.	Ⓐ Ⓑ Ⓒ Ⓓ
6.	Ⓐ Ⓑ Ⓒ Ⓓ	12.	Ⓐ Ⓑ Ⓒ Ⓓ	18.	Ⓐ Ⓑ Ⓒ Ⓓ	24.	Ⓐ Ⓑ Ⓒ Ⓓ	30.	Ⓐ Ⓑ Ⓒ Ⓓ

HUMAN BODY AND HEALTH

LEARNING OBJECTIVES

- Skeleton system
- Nervous system
- Sensory organs
- Balance diet
- Communicable and Non-communicable Diseases

MULTIPLE CHOICE QUESTIONS

Direction: Select the correct option.

1. Which joint allows the maximum movement?
   (A) Gliding joint
   (B) Hinge joint
   (C) Pivot joint
   (D) Ball and socket joint
2. Muscles are attached to the bones with the fibre called ________.
   (A) Ribs
   (B) Ligaments
   (C) Tendons
   (D) Bone marrow
3. Which muscles are under our control?
   (A) Muscles attached to the alimentary canal
   (B) Cardiac muscles
   (C) Muscles attached to our skeleton
   (D) None of these
4. The joints in the skull are ________.
   (A) Voluntary (B) Involuntary
   (C) Movable (D) Immovable
5. The largest bone in our body is ________.
   (A) Sternum bone
   (B) Femur (Thigh bone)
   (C) Girdle bones
   (D) Forearm bones
6. Bones are made up of:
   (A) Calcium (B) Potassium
   (C) Sodium (D) Iron
7. Rotation of arm in a full circle is possible due to ________.
   (A) Hinge joint
   (B) Pivot joint
   (C) Gliding joint
   (D) Ball and socket joint
8. Gliding joint is present in ________.
   (A) Girdle (B) Arms
   (C) Legs (D) Wrist
9. Stripes of tough connective tissues that hold bones together are known as ________.
   (A) Tendons
   (B) Smooth muscles
   (C) Straight muscles
   (D) Ligaments
10. Which of the following statements is true?
    (A) Bones are mode of iron.
    (B) Humerus bone is present in the thigh.
    (C) Locomotion is a type of movement.
    (D) The strongest muscle is the eye ball muscle.

11. Which of these diseases affect the joints?
(A) Malaria (B) Tetanus
(C) Arthritis (D) Fracture

12. The part of the human brain which is an important relay station for the sensory impulses and is also the origin of many of the involuntary acts of the eye such as the narrowing of the pupil in bright light is __________.
(A) Hypothalamus
(B) Midbrain
(C) Corpus callosum
(D) Cerebellum

13. The nervous system develops from which germ layer?
(A) Ectoderm
(B) Mesoderm
(C) Endoderm
(D) None of these

14. Which of the following is an example of striated tissue?
(A) Muscle (B) Nervous
(C) Epithelial (D) Connective

15. What type of tissue is bone tissue?
(A) Muscle (B) Nervous
(C) Epithelial (D) Connective

16. The disease resulting from lack of energy and protein in the diet is called _________.
(A) Malnutrition
(B) Scurvy
(C) Beri beri
(D) All of these

17. Rickets in children and osteomalacia in adults are deficiency diseases of _______.
(A) Iron (B) Vitamin A
(C) Iodine (D) Calcium

18. Which of the following are not nutrients?
(A) Proteins and carbohydrates
(B) Vitamins and minerals
(C) Dal and rice
(D) Both (A) and (B)

19. Which of the following helps the body get rid of undigested waste?
(A) Vitamins (B) Roughage
(C) Proteins (D) Minerals

20. Communicable diseases are also known as _________.
(A) Infectious
(B) Non-infectious
(C) Both (A) and (B)
(D) None of these

21. Diseases like malaria and dengue are spread by _________.
(A) Sneezing
(B) Coughing
(C) Direct contact
(D) Mosquito bites

22. Which of the following foods is a good source of fiber?
(A) A piece of pie
(B) Scrambled eggs
(C) Potato skin
(D) A cup of yogurt

23. A person who does not eat meat should _________.
(A) Eat less from the milk, yogurt, and cheese group.
(B) Substitute pasta for meat.
(C) Eat additional servings from all of the other groups.
(D) Substitute beans and nuts for meat.

24. Which of the following nutrients is responsible for strengthening muscles, bones, and teeth?
(A) Vitamins
(B) Minerals
(C) Fats
(D) Carbohydrates

25. Which of the following is not a recommended way to maintain a healthy diet?
(A) Eating a varied diet
(B) Avoiding foods high in fats and calories

(C) Avoiding too much sugar
(D) Eliminating sodium from your diet

26. Which of the following behaviour is part of a healthy eating plan?
    (A) Saumya sometimes eats cold spaghetti or leftover pizza for breakfast.
    (B) Ananya likes to eat lot of fruits and vegetables along with milk.
    (C) Sumit skips breakfast when he is late for school.
    (D) Anubhav counts fruit pie and sugared drinks that contain some fruit as his daily fruit servings.

27. What is common between bread, jam and potato chips?
    (A) Rich in fat
    (B) Rich in carbohydrate and protein
    (C) Rich in carbohydrate
    (D) Rich in fiber

28. Foods rich in carbohydrates are _______.
    (A) Spinach, onion, ginger, tomato
    (B) Potato, wheat, maize, sugarcane
    (C) Mango, papaya, orange, banana
    (D) Meat, fish, egg, pulses

29. If a person eats too much of food rich in fat and does no physical work, it leads to _______.
    (A) Malnutrition
    (B) Vitamin deficiency
    (C) Night blindness
    (D) Obesity

30. Diseases that occur due to lack of nutrients for over a long period are called _______.
    (A) Infectious diseases
    (B) Deficiency diseases
    (C) Food lacking diseases
    (D) Obesity

HOTS (ACHIEVERS SECTION)

31. The following is a diagram of the human digestive system.

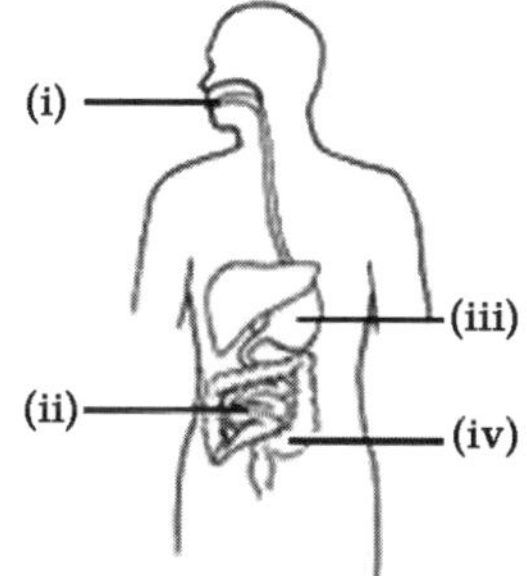

Which number shows the place where food mixes with acids to help break it down into parts that can be absorbed?
    (A) (i) (B) (iii)
    (C) (ii) (D) (iv)

32. Look at the given diagram carefully.

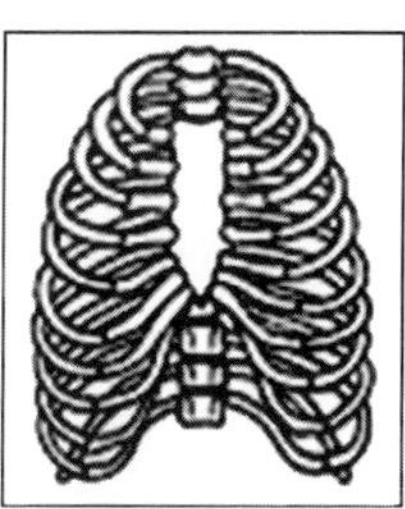

Which are the organs that the above given bones protect?

(i) stomach
(ii) lungs
(iii) liver
(iv) heart

(A) Only (i) and (ii)
(B) Only (i) and (iii)
(C) Only (ii) and (iii)
(D) Only (ii) and (iv)

33. In what ways are the thigh muscles and arm muscles similar?

(i)	They crate movement by contracting and relaxing.
(ii)	They work in pairs.
(iii)	They are attached to the bones.

(A) Only (i) and (iii)
(B) Only (i) and (ii)
(C) Only (ii) and (iii)
(D) (i), (ii) and (iii)

34. Judith compared a set of four pictures.

From these pictures, she concluded that ______.

(A) The skeleton determines the body shape
(B) The skeleton protects the delicate organs in the body
(C) The skeleton moves with the help of muscles and joints
(D) All of these

35. What enables us to swing our arms as shown in the picture?

(A) Ball and socket joint
(B) Pivot joint
(C) Hinge joint
(D) Sliding joint

36. Below is a clinical observation report of a person showing some clinical indications. Read the report and answer the following questions.

Clinical Report
Name of the patient: Mr. Shah Age: 55 Sex: M **Symptoms:** Severe Back pain Two fractures in last 6 months Stooped walking posture

A. What could be the reason behind the symptoms?
B. How can food modification help Mr. Shah?

	A	B
(A)	Scurvy (Vitamin C deficiency)	Eating citrus fruits
(B)	Iodine Deficiency	Eating iodised salt
(C)	Calcium deficiency	Eating products like milk, poultry, meat, and green leafy vegetables
(D)	Vitamin A deficiency	Eating lots of green leafy vegetables

37. Match the following:

List I		List II	
A	Refrigeration means	1	when food is boiled to kill bacteria
B	Canning is	2	to take out water from the food item
C	Dehydration is	3	to keep the products in a refrigerator

	A	B	C
(A)	2	3	1
(B)	3	1	2
(C)	1	2	3
(D)	3	2	1

38. Read the statements and choose the correct options.

Statement A: In chemical preservation, soil is used to conserve the food items.

Statement B: We should pack the food with extra care while we are going on travel.

Statement C: We can pack all the food items together in a box.

Statement D: Airtight tiffin's are used to pack clothes.

(A) TFFT (B) FFTT
(C) FTFF (D) TFTF

39. Read the passage and answer the questions below: When there is lack of availability of food, this situation is called famine. Sometimes, the volcanic eruptions, floods and droughts are the reason for it. These natural calamities destroy the crops. Sometimes improper storage of food spoils it and brings the situation of famine, there have been many deaths due to lack of food in many years. Our body needs all the vitamins and minerals for proper functioning and growth. When it does not receive some nutrients, it falls prey to diseases. Lack of nutrition is called malnutrition. There are many diseases such as kwashiorkor, marasmus and scurvy which are malnutrition diseases. How do natural calamities bring the famine?

(A) They destroy the crops
(B) They eat the food
(C) They store the food
(D) All of these

40. Read the passage and answer the questions below: When there is lack of availability of food, this situation is called famine. Sometimes, the volcanic eruptions, floods and droughts are the reason for it. These natural calamities destroy the crops. Sometimes improper storage of food spoils it and brings the situation of famine, there have been many deaths due to lack of food in many years. Our body needs all the vitamins and minerals for proper functioning and growth. When it does not receive some nutrients, it falls prey to diseases. Lack of nutrition is called malnutrition. There are many diseases such as kwashiorkor, marasmus and scurvy which are malnutrition diseases. Our body needs oil the vitamins and nutrients in proper amount.

(A) True (B) False
(C) Partially true (D) None of these

Darken Your Choice with HB Pencil

1.	Ⓐ	Ⓑ	Ⓒ	Ⓓ	9.	Ⓐ	Ⓑ	Ⓒ	Ⓓ	17.	Ⓐ	Ⓑ	Ⓒ	Ⓓ	25	Ⓐ	Ⓑ	Ⓒ	Ⓓ	33.	Ⓐ	Ⓑ	Ⓒ	Ⓓ
2.	Ⓐ	Ⓑ	Ⓒ	Ⓓ	10.	Ⓐ	Ⓑ	Ⓒ	Ⓓ	18.	Ⓐ	Ⓑ	Ⓒ	Ⓓ	26.	Ⓐ	Ⓑ	Ⓒ	Ⓓ	34.	Ⓐ	Ⓑ	Ⓒ	Ⓓ
3.	Ⓐ	Ⓑ	Ⓒ	Ⓓ	11.	Ⓐ	Ⓑ	Ⓒ	Ⓓ	19.	Ⓐ	Ⓑ	Ⓒ	Ⓓ	27.	Ⓐ	Ⓑ	Ⓒ	Ⓓ	35.	Ⓐ	Ⓑ	Ⓒ	Ⓓ
4.	Ⓐ	Ⓑ	Ⓒ	Ⓓ	12.	Ⓐ	Ⓑ	Ⓒ	Ⓓ	20.	Ⓐ	Ⓑ	Ⓒ	Ⓓ	28.	Ⓐ	Ⓑ	Ⓒ	Ⓓ	36.	Ⓐ	Ⓑ	Ⓒ	Ⓓ
5.	Ⓐ	Ⓑ	Ⓒ	Ⓓ	13.	Ⓐ	Ⓑ	Ⓒ	Ⓓ	21.	Ⓐ	Ⓑ	Ⓒ	Ⓓ	29.	Ⓐ	Ⓑ	Ⓒ	Ⓓ	37.	Ⓐ	Ⓑ	Ⓒ	Ⓓ
6.	Ⓐ	Ⓑ	Ⓒ	Ⓓ	14.	Ⓐ	Ⓑ	Ⓒ	Ⓓ	22.	Ⓐ	Ⓑ	Ⓒ	Ⓓ	30.	Ⓐ	Ⓑ	Ⓒ	Ⓓ	38.	Ⓐ	Ⓑ	Ⓒ	Ⓓ
7.	Ⓐ	Ⓑ	Ⓒ	Ⓓ	15.	Ⓐ	Ⓑ	Ⓒ	Ⓓ	23.	Ⓐ	Ⓑ	Ⓒ	Ⓓ	31.	Ⓐ	Ⓑ	Ⓒ	Ⓓ	39.	Ⓐ	Ⓑ	Ⓒ	Ⓓ
8.	Ⓐ	Ⓑ	Ⓒ	Ⓓ	16.	Ⓐ	Ⓑ	Ⓒ	Ⓓ	24.	Ⓐ	Ⓑ	Ⓒ	Ⓓ	32.	Ⓐ	Ⓑ	Ⓒ	Ⓓ	40.	Ⓐ	Ⓑ	Ⓒ	Ⓓ

PLANT LIFE

LEARNING OBJECTIVES

- Photosynthesis
- Reproduction in plants
- Vegetative propagation

MULTIPLE CHOICE QUESTIONS

Direction: Select the correct option.

1. What signals show that a tree is preparing for the winter?
   (A) The days become colder
   (B) The weather becomes dry
   (C) There are more rainy days
   (D) There are fewer hours of sunlight
2. Why do the leaves of trees change colour in the fall?
   (A) The tree has less chlorophyll
   (B) The tree has less water
   (C) The tree has no leaves
   (D) The tree is growing quickly before the winter sets in
3. If a mango sapling grows too near to the parent tree, it ________.
   (A) May not be able to spread its branches
   (B) May not get enough water
   (C) May not get sufficient sunlight
   (D) All of these
4. What do the roots of plants absorb from soil?
   (A) Nutrients
   (B) Water
   (C) Both (A) and (B)
   (D) None of these
5. The method in which the stem of a plant is used to produce a new plant without detaching it from the plant is called ________.
   (A) Cutting
   (B) Layering
   (C) Budding
   (D) Both (A) and (B)
6. Where do the tribal people get their food from?
   (A) From trees
   (B) By hunting animals
   (C) From groceries
   (D) Both (A) and (B)
7. From which part of the plant does Bryophyllum grows?
   (A) Leaves
   (B) Stems
   (C) Roots
   (D) None of these
8. Plants that need clayey soil to grow well are ________.
   (A) Tea and coffee
   (B) Jowar and bajra
   (C) Wheat and gram
   (D) Rice and jute

9. The seed with thick fibrous outer covering is ___________.
   (A) Neem (B) Coconut
   (C) Papaya (D) Lemon
10. Which part of the seed stores food?
    (A) Plumule (B) Shoot
    (C) Root (D) Cotyledon
11. Which part of the embryo grows first?
    (A) Cotyledon (B) Plumule
    (C) Radicle (D) Leaves
12. What happens if seeds are kept under water?
    (A) Seeds will germinate
    (B) Seed will not germinate
    (C) Water stops entering into the seed
    (D) Seed gives rise to seedling
13. What kind of crop is apple?
    (A) Kharif (B) Rabi
    (C) Spongy (D) None of these
14. What kind of crop is peanut?
    (A) Kharif (B) Rabi
    (C) Spongy (D) None of these
15. How is a tea plant propagated?
    (A) From cutting
    (B) From seeds
    (C) From leaves
    (D) By watering the ground
16. How has deforestation affected the wildlife?
    (A) There are species which are near extinction.
    (B) Animals do not have shelter.
    (C) Animals do not have food.
    (D) All of these
17. Which of the following is the best suited condition for seeds to germinate?
    (A) (B)
    (C) (D)
18. Which of the following shows the correct match of seed and its mode of dispersal?
    (A) 
    Explosion
    (B)
    Water
    (C) 
    Animal
    (D) 
    Wind
19. Which of the following statements is true?
    (A) Sunflower plant is an insectivorous plant.
    (B) Some plants can grow completely under water.
    (C) Best example of climbers is rose plant.
    (D) Roots of some plants are also found above the ground.
20. From which part of the plant can sugarcane be grown?
    (A) Roots
    (B) Stems
    (C) Leaves
    (D) Both (A) and (B)
21. The development process of a seed is called ___________.
    (A) Photosynthesis
    (B) Germination
    (C) Transpiration
    (D) Dormancy
22. What is the primary method by which horsetail spores are dispersed?
    (A) Water
    (B) Wind
    (C) Insects
    (D) Grazing animals

23. Which of the reproductive structures in the following figures are pollinated by wind?

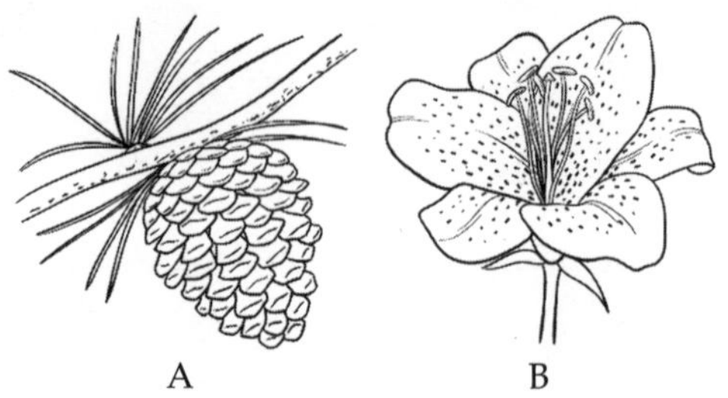

(A) A
(B) B
(C) Both (A) and (B)
(D) Neither (A) nor (B)

24. What do farmers add to the soil to make it fertile?
(A) Manure
(B) Chemical fertilizers
(C) Both (A) and (B)
(D) Neither (A) nor (B)

25. The joining of a sperm and an egg during sexual reproduction is called ____________.
(A) Pollination
(B) Germination
(C) Fertilization
(D) Flowering

HOTS (ACHIEVERS SECTION)

26. The following are pictures of leaves found on different plants.

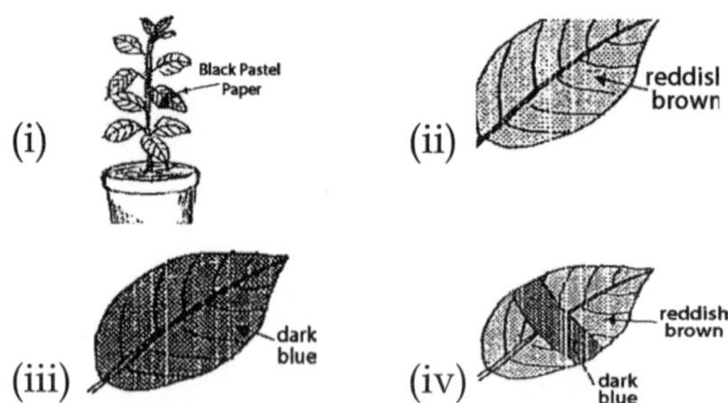

Which of these plants would be found in an ecosystem with heavy snowfall?
(A) Plant (i)
(B) Plant (iii)
(C) Plant (iv)
(D) Plant (ii)

27. During long periods of dry weather many plants have a special adaptation that helps to keep them from losing water. What is this adaptation?
(A) They make seeds.
(B) They grow more leaves.
(C) They get shorter.
(D) Their leaves curl up.

28. Read the sentences carefully and find The True/False

Water helps in seed dispersal of some plants.

The seed dispersal in palm trees takes place with the help of water.

Seeds can travel only a short distance while travelling through water.
(A) TFF
(B) TTT
(C) TFT
(D) TTF

29. New buildings are constructing day by day due to increase in population. As a result forest are cutting down. What can be the consequences of this?
(A) Wild life will be destroyed.
(B) Wild life and the life of tribal people will get destroyed.
(C) We will get free land to build luxurious houses.
(D) Both (A) and (B)

30. Rahul and Vijay went to a park to play. There were many plants in the park. Some plants were small and some big. Suddenly while playing Vijay tried to uproot a plant. Rahul stopped him from doing so. What according to you is the correct reason behind this?

(A) Plants are very beautiful.

(B) Some plants such as money plant provide us money.

(C) Plants provide us fresh air, many fruits and vegetable which we use to eat.

(D) All of these

Darken Your Choice with HB Pencil

1.	Ⓐ Ⓑ Ⓒ Ⓓ	7.	Ⓐ Ⓑ Ⓒ Ⓓ	13.	Ⓐ Ⓑ Ⓒ Ⓓ	19	Ⓐ Ⓑ Ⓒ Ⓓ	25.	Ⓐ Ⓑ Ⓒ Ⓓ
2.	Ⓐ Ⓑ Ⓒ Ⓓ	8.	Ⓐ Ⓑ Ⓒ Ⓓ	14.	Ⓐ Ⓑ Ⓒ Ⓓ	20.	Ⓐ Ⓑ Ⓒ Ⓓ	26.	Ⓐ Ⓑ Ⓒ Ⓓ
3.	Ⓐ Ⓑ Ⓒ Ⓓ	9.	Ⓐ Ⓑ Ⓒ Ⓓ	15.	Ⓐ Ⓑ Ⓒ Ⓓ	21.	Ⓐ Ⓑ Ⓒ Ⓓ	27.	Ⓐ Ⓑ Ⓒ Ⓓ
4.	Ⓐ Ⓑ Ⓒ Ⓓ	10.	Ⓐ Ⓑ Ⓒ Ⓓ	16.	Ⓐ Ⓑ Ⓒ Ⓓ	22.	Ⓐ Ⓑ Ⓒ Ⓓ	28.	Ⓐ Ⓑ Ⓒ Ⓓ
5.	Ⓐ Ⓑ Ⓒ Ⓓ	11.	Ⓐ Ⓑ Ⓒ Ⓓ	17.	Ⓐ Ⓑ Ⓒ Ⓓ	23.	Ⓐ Ⓑ Ⓒ Ⓓ	29.	Ⓐ Ⓑ Ⓒ Ⓓ
6.	Ⓐ Ⓑ Ⓒ Ⓓ	12.	Ⓐ Ⓑ Ⓒ Ⓓ	18.	Ⓐ Ⓑ Ⓒ Ⓓ	24.	Ⓐ Ⓑ Ⓒ Ⓓ	30.	Ⓐ Ⓑ Ⓒ Ⓓ

NATURAL RESOURCES AND CALAMITIES

LEARNING OBJECTIVES

- ➤ Soil and its types
- ➤ Rocks and its types
- ➤ Indian Heritage
- ➤ Soil erosion and soil conservation
- ➤ Natural calamities

MULTIPLE CHOICE QUESTIONS

Direction: Select the correct option.

1. A dark-coloured substance formed from dead remains of plants and animals is called _________.
   (A) Gravel (B) Humus
   (C) Loam (D) Clay

2. Which of the following layers of soil supports plant growth?
   (A) Bedrock (B) Subsoil
   (C) Topsoil (D) None of these

3. The water holding capacity is highest in _________.
   (A) Loamy soil
   (B) Sandy soil
   (C) Clayey soil
   (D) None of these

4. Why is organic matter (humus) an important part of soil?
   (A) It helps to improve water infiltration.
   (B) It can break down organic pollutants.
   (C) It converts nitrogen in the air into nitrates used by plants.
   (D) It is rich in nutrients, which is important for fertility.

5. What is soil erosion?
   (A) It is the process by which soil is formed.
   (B) A harmful process that involves the removal and transport of soil by wind and water.
   (C) A natural method of filtering harmful pollutants.
   (D) A process often referred to as the greenhouse effect.

6. Which of the following factors is/are responsible for the depletion of the world's natural resources?
   i. Increasing numbers of vehicles in use.
   ii. An increase in the human population.
   iii. The greater use of biodegradable products.
   (A) i only
   (B) Both i and ii
   (C) iii only
   (D) Both ii and iii

7. Terrace farming helps in _________.
   (A) Reducing soil erosion by using non-arable land.
   (B) Reducing soil erosion by deforestation.
   (C) Reducing soil erosion by water.
   (D) Reducing soil erosion by overgrazing.

8. A flash flood is a flood that ________.
   (A) Is caused by heavy rain rather than from the flooding of a river
   (B) Occurs in urban areas
   (C) Occurs suddenly and unexpectedly and for a short duration
   (D) Is caused by the blocking of drains

9. Which of the following is an environmental consequence of floods?
   (A) Dispersal of weed species
   (B) Erosion of soil
   (C) Release of pollutants into waterways
   (D) All of these

10. Coal, when burnt, produces ________.
   (A) Chemical potential energy
   (B) Thermal energy
   (C) Kinetic energy
   (D) Electric energy

11. Which out of the following is derived from the ocean waters?
   (A) Limestone
   (B) Sandstone
   (C) Cobalt
   (D) Bromine

12. Where is the largest solar plant of India located?
   (A) Gujarat
   (B) Rajasthan
   (C) Maharashtra
   (D) Odisha

13. Which energy source below best fits the information in the table?

   Type of energy: ________

Advantages	Disadvantages
Simple to transport	Air and water pollution
Supply available for 250 more years	Habitat destruction

   (A) Wind
   (B) Hydro
   (C) Coal
   (D) Tidal

14. _____ is the major raw material for biogas.
   (A) Plant leaves
   (B) Cow dung
   (C) Mud
   (D) Grass

15. Which one of the following is not a fossil fuel?
   (A) Natural gas
   (B) Petrol
   (C) Coal
   (D) Uranium

16. The death of the last individual of a species is called ________.
   (A) Extinction
   (B) Clad
   (C) Neither (A) nor (B)
   (D) Species diversity

17. A place where an earthquake originates is called the ________.
   (A) Focus
   (B) Tsunami
   (C) Fault Line
   (D) Epicenter

18. ________ helps the environment by slowing down the rate at which we have to burn garbage or put it in landfills.
   (A) Recycling
   (B) Reusing
   (C) Reducing
   (D) None of these

19. If an earthquake occurs, which of the following you should not do?
   (A) If you are on a beach, get into the sea.
   (B) If you are indoors, stay in and get under a desk or a table.
   (C) If you are outdoors, stay away from trees and buildings.
   (D) All of these

20. Which of the following is a non-renewable source of energy?
   (A) Water
   (B) Coal
   (C) Petroleum
   (D) Both (B) and (C)
21. Which of these is not an igneous rock?
   (A) Basalt
   (B) Granite
   (C) Obsidian
   (D) Sandstone
22. What is measured on the Richter Scale from 1 to 8?
   (A) The intensity of an earthquake
   (B) The intensity of a volcano
   (C) The intensity of tsunami
   (D) The intensity of flood
23. The burning of fossil fuels does not release __________.
   (A) Potential energy
   (B) Light energy
   (C) Sound energy
   (D) Heat energy
24. There are many places where wave energy can be produced. The best place to generate energy from waves is __________.
   (A) The sea
   (B) A reservoir
   (C) A big river
   (D) A lake
25. Floods can be prevented by _________.
   (A) Afforestation
   (B) Cutting the forests
   (C) Tilling the land
   (D) Removing the top soil
26. A Tsunami event can begin with a drawdown or retreat if the _________ of the wave arrives first.
   (A) Top
   (B) Right side
   (C) Left side
   (D) Trough
27. Which natural disaster is the most common in the United States of America and Australia?
   (A) Tsunami
   (B) Flooding
   (C) Tornado
   (D) None of these
28. One of the world's worst-ever volcanic eruptions took place 74,000 years ago on an island in which Asian country?
   (A) Indonesia
   (B) Iran
   (C) Japan
   (D) None of these
29. In ______, we leave a mixture in a jar undisturbed for some time so that impurities get settled at the bottom and then slowly pour clear water into another jar.
   (A) Filtration
   (B) Evaporation
   (C) Decantation
   (D) Condensation
30. Soil is formed from rocks by the process of ____ that occurs due to effects of ____, ____, etc. Select the option that will correctly complete the given sentence.
   (A) Erosion, temperature, wind
   (B) Erosion, microorganisms, water
   (C) Weathering, erosion, pollution
   (D) Weathering, water, wind

HOTS (ACHIEVERS SECTION)

31. Recently, City A experienced a natural calamity. The children from a school in City A tried defining various natural calamities.

Student	Calamity	Features
A	Earthquake	A sudden movement in the Earth's crust
	Tsunami	A huge ocean wave caused by underwater earthquakes, volcanic eruptions, or slumping
	Landslide	A large mass of soil or rock that slides down a volcano or mountain
	Hurricane	Wind that blows at speeds greater than 119 kilometers (74 miles) per hour
B	Earthquake	A sudden movement in the Earth's crust
	Tsunami	A huge ocean wave caused by underwater earthquakes, volcanic eruptions, or slumping
	Landslide	A large mass of soil or rock that slides down a volcano or mountain
	Tornado	Wind that blows at speeds greater than 119 kilometers (74 miles) per hour
C	Earthquake	A sudden movement in the Earth's crust
	Slumping	A huge ocean wave caused by underwater earthquakes
	Landslide	A large mass of soil or rock that slides down a volcano or mountain
	Hurricane	Wind that blows at speeds greater than 119 kilometers (74 miles) per hour

I. Which student has defined the natural calamities correctly?

II. How many of the listed natural calamities are related to the movement of the Earth?

	I	II
(A)	A	2
(B)	B	3
(C)	A	3
(D)	C	3

32. The given picture shows that air ______.

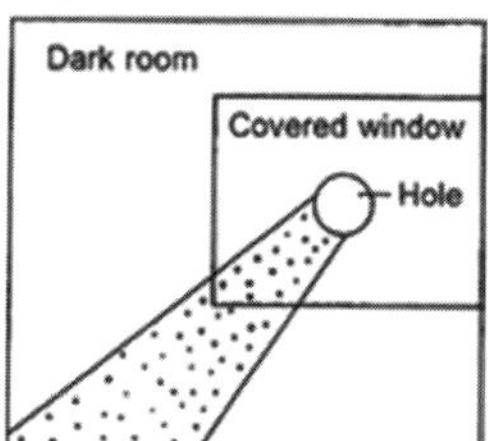

(A) Has mass
(B) Occupies space
(C) Contains dust
(D) Gives shape to things

33. Select the correct option regarding natural resources.
    (A) They can never be exhausted.
    (B) They are obtained from soil only.
    (C) Non-mineral resources include air and water.
    (D) Some of the natural resources are harmful to us.

34. Three glasses P, Q and R having equal amount of water were taken at room temperature and equal amount of salt was added to each one of them. After that, P was cooled, Q was heated and R was left undisturbed. Water in which glass will now taste most salty?

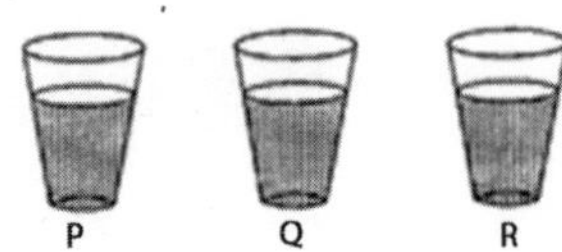

    (A) P
    (B) Q
    (C) R
    (D) All will taste the same

35. The rock X can be _____.

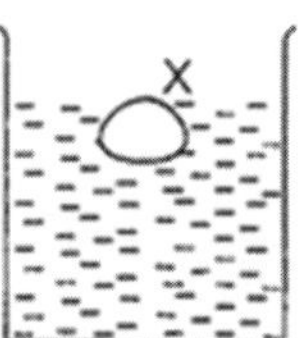

    (A) Granite   (B) Pumice
    (C) Marble   (D) Shale

Darken Your Choice with HB Pencil

1.	Ⓐ	Ⓑ	Ⓒ	Ⓓ	8.	Ⓐ	Ⓑ	Ⓒ	Ⓓ	15.	Ⓐ	Ⓑ	Ⓒ	Ⓓ	22	Ⓐ	Ⓑ	Ⓒ	Ⓓ	29.	Ⓐ	Ⓑ	Ⓒ	Ⓓ
2.	Ⓐ	Ⓑ	Ⓒ	Ⓓ	9.	Ⓐ	Ⓑ	Ⓒ	Ⓓ	16.	Ⓐ	Ⓑ	Ⓒ	Ⓓ	23.	Ⓐ	Ⓑ	Ⓒ	Ⓓ	30.	Ⓐ	Ⓑ	Ⓒ	Ⓓ
3.	Ⓐ	Ⓑ	Ⓒ	Ⓓ	10.	Ⓐ	Ⓑ	Ⓒ	Ⓓ	17.	Ⓐ	Ⓑ	Ⓒ	Ⓓ	24.	Ⓐ	Ⓑ	Ⓒ	Ⓓ	31.	Ⓐ	Ⓑ	Ⓒ	Ⓓ
4.	Ⓐ	Ⓑ	Ⓒ	Ⓓ	11.	Ⓐ	Ⓑ	Ⓒ	Ⓓ	18.	Ⓐ	Ⓑ	Ⓒ	Ⓓ	25.	Ⓐ	Ⓑ	Ⓒ	Ⓓ	32.	Ⓐ	Ⓑ	Ⓒ	Ⓓ
5.	Ⓐ	Ⓑ	Ⓒ	Ⓓ	12.	Ⓐ	Ⓑ	Ⓒ	Ⓓ	19.	Ⓐ	Ⓑ	Ⓒ	Ⓓ	26.	Ⓐ	Ⓑ	Ⓒ	Ⓓ	33.	Ⓐ	Ⓑ	Ⓒ	Ⓓ
6.	Ⓐ	Ⓑ	Ⓒ	Ⓓ	13.	Ⓐ	Ⓑ	Ⓒ	Ⓓ	20.	Ⓐ	Ⓑ	Ⓒ	Ⓓ	27.	Ⓐ	Ⓑ	Ⓒ	Ⓓ	34.	Ⓐ	Ⓑ	Ⓒ	Ⓓ
7.	Ⓐ	Ⓑ	Ⓒ	Ⓓ	14.	Ⓐ	Ⓑ	Ⓒ	Ⓓ	21.	Ⓐ	Ⓑ	Ⓒ	Ⓓ	28.	Ⓐ	Ⓑ	Ⓒ	Ⓓ	35.	Ⓐ	Ⓑ	Ⓒ	Ⓓ

WATER

LEARNING OBJECTIVES

- Water as a source of life
- Properties of water
- Water pollution
- Water purification

MULTIPLE CHOICE QUESTIONS

Direction: Select the correct option.

1. What is rainwater harvesting?
   (A) Soring ground water by not using water from the well
   (B) Allowing water to go into rivers and lakes
   (C) To stop growing crops to save water
   (D) Collecting rainwater and storing it for later use

2. At which temperature does water turn into ice?
   (A) 33°F
   (B) 32°F
   (C) 35°F
   (D) 0°F

3. Water continually circulates between the Earth's surface and atmosphere. This process is called ____________.
   (A) Evaporation
   (B) Water cycle
   (C) Condensation
   (D) Transpiration

4. What is the main reason behind the downward flow of water?
   (A) Gravity
   (B) Volume
   (C) Surface tension
   (D) Density

5. Whether an object sinks or floats depends upon its ____________.
   (A) Volume
   (B) Surface tension
   (C) Gravity
   (D) Density

6. Which of these diseases are more prevalent in areas with poor sanitary conditions?
   (A) Insect borne
   (B) Water borne
   (C) Bacteria borne
   (D) Virus borne

7. The picture shows a tourist place in Hampi. This is a traditional well with multiple steps around it. The technique of pulling water with rope and basket is not much seen here. What is it called?

(A) Wells
(B) Piaaos
(C) Baolis
(D) Amphitheatre

8. Drainage water is also used for irrigation. It is a ____________.

(A) Surface water source
(B) Non-conventional source
(C) Dirty water
(D) Ground water

9. Look at the following picture carefully and find out which of the labelled parts is called filtrate?

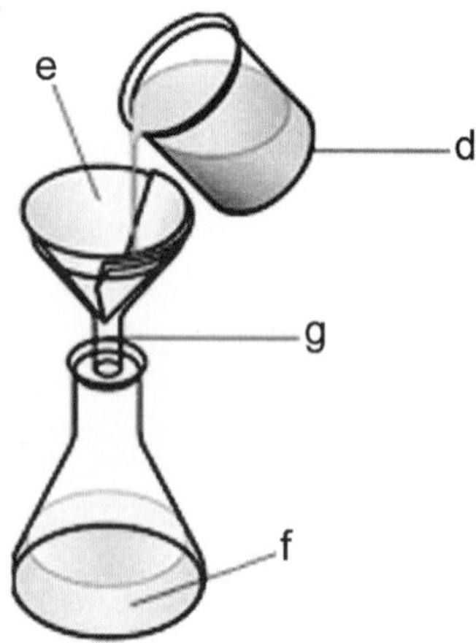

(A) e (B) d
(C) g (D) f

10. In which of the following ways can we use water?

(A) Use water collected from rain to wash vegetables
(B) Collect water from tap leaks to cook
(C) Use water that is drained out from the washing machine to wash the toilet
(D) Use water that is drained out from the washing machine to water plants

11. When a mixture of salt + sugar + vinegar + lemon juice + soda was added into water, it resulted in the formation of a ____________.

(A) Mixture in which all ingredients are mixed except soda that forms separate layer
(B) Soluble mixture
(C) Layers of different mixtures
(D) None of these

12. What is depicted in the image given below?

(A) Water cycle
(B) Waterwheel
(C) Merry-go-round
(D) Water pump

13. Look at the following picture carefully and find out what processes are taking place?

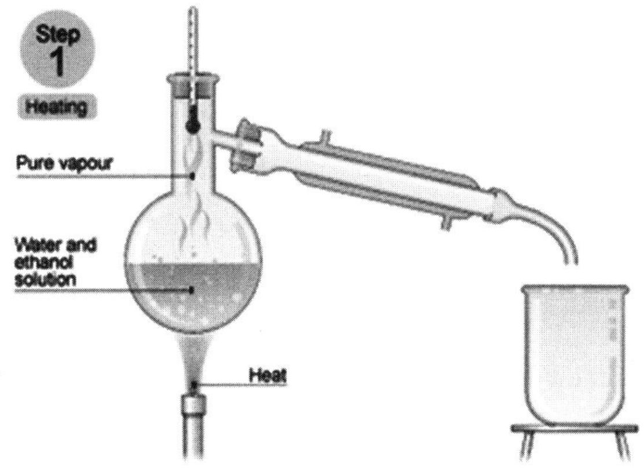

(A) Condensation and filtration
(B) Evaporation and condensation
(C) Sedimentation and decantation
(D) Evaporation and decantation

14. Water's high surface tension allows it to do which of the following?
(A) It gives water the ability to bead on objects
(B) It gives water a sticky property
(C) It gives water the ability to circulate upward on and through objects
(D) All of these

15. How many calories are absorbed/released when 1 gram of water freezes or melts?
(A) 680
(B) 550
(C) 80
(D) 580

16. Why doesn't the temperature of water increase as it is undergoing a phase change?
(A) Because the energy is consumed to break free the water's hydrogen bonds
(B) Because the absorbed energy serves to cool the water as it undergoes the change, therefore making it impossible for it to increase its temperature
(C) Because the energy is always released to the surrounding atmosphere as it undergoes a phase change
(D) Because energy and temperature have nothing to do with the various phase changes of water

17. As water vapour condenses, energy is ________ and it ________ the surrounding atmosphere.
(A) Released; heats
(B) Absorbed; cools
(C) Absorbed; heats
(D) Released; cools

18. What is the greatest significance of latent heat?
(A) Its release serves to break down water's hydrogen bonds
(B) It allows water vapour to serve as a large reservoir of heat in the Earth's atmosphere
(C) Massive amounts of it are stored in glacial ice, and as it melts it will serve to increase global temperatures significantly
(D) Its release serves to break down water's oxygen bonds

19. What is the correct definition of solubility?
(A) The ability of solid particles to disperse throughout a liquid continuous phase
(B) The ability of a solute to dissolve into a solvent
(C) The rate at which a solute dissolves into a solvent
(D) The ability of immiscible liquid droplets to disperse within a second liquid phase

20. Read the following paragraph and arrange the following mentioned events (A, B, C, D) in the order in which they took place.

"Titanic was a British passenger liner that sank in the North Atlantic Ocean on 15 April, 1912 after colliding with an iceberg on 14 April, 1912. Some 1500 people perished."

(A) The ship sank
(B) The fast moving ship hit an iceberg
(C) Ship was floating in the ocean
(D) The ship got pierced from one corner after hitting the iceberg and the water from the ocean started entering the ship

(A) ABCD (B) CBDA
(C) BADA (D) CADA

21. Aquatic plants are also known as ______.
(A) Watercress
(B) Wild rice
(C) Hydrophytes
(D) Water-growing plants

22. Keerti wanted to check the solubility of some solids like sugar, salt, chalk powder, and saw dust in water. She took four beakers containing equal amount of water. Then she added the solids to each beaker, stirred the contents with a spoon and waited for some time. What did she observe?

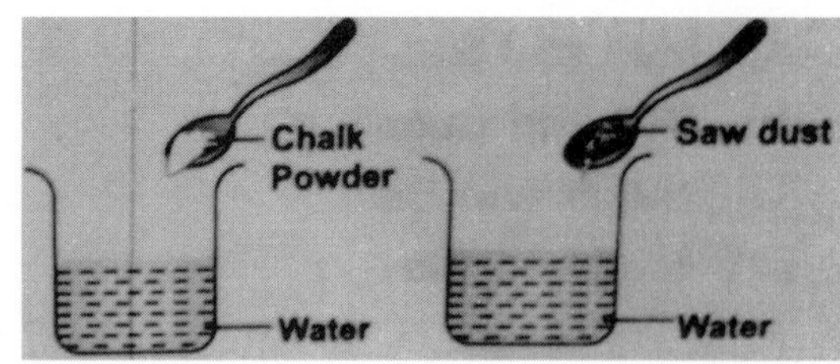

(A) Sugar, salt, chalk powder and saw dust are soluble in water
(B) Sugar and chalk powder are soluble in water while salt and saw are insoluble
(C) Sugar and salt are soluble in water while chalk powder and saw dust are insoluble
(D) Sugar, salt, and chalk powder are soluble in water while saw dust is insoluble

23. Insoluble impurities may be removed from water by ______.
(A) Evaporation
(B) Sedimentation
(C) Chlorination
(D) Distillation

24. The process by which an insoluble impurity is separated from a liquid by passing the mixture through filter paper is called ______.
(A) Filtration
(B) Sedimentation
(C) Chlorination
(D) Distillation

25. This form of water is called the purest form of water and is used in car batteries ______.
(A) Boiled water
(B) RO water
(C) Filtered water
(D) Distilled water

HOTS (ACHIEVERS SECTION)

26. Study the given table to answer the following question.

S.No.	State	Change
I.	A substance changes from a gas phase to a liquid phase and particles move closer	Freezing
II.	A substance changes from a liquid to a gas (or vapour) naturally and particles move apart	Evaporation
III.	A substance changes from a solid to the gas phase and particles move apart	Melting
IV.	A substance changes from a liquid to a gas (or vapour) naturally and particles move closer	Evaporation

Which option is correctly paired?
(A) Evaporation - II
(B) Condensation - I
(C) Sublimation - III
(D) Evaporation -IV

27. Look at the following water cycle.

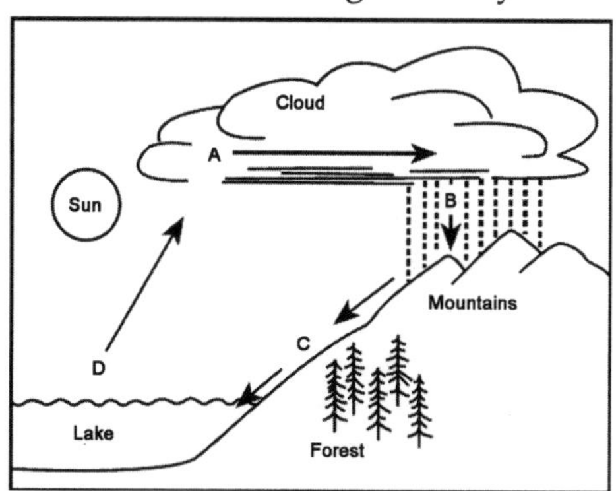

Which process is occurring at point D?
(A) Condensation to evaporation
(B) Evaporation to condensation
(C) Condensation to precipitation
(D) Run off to evaporation

28. A plastic cup containing a wooden block is floating in a pan of water as shown in the diagram below.
A. If another wood block is placed in the cup, what will happen to the level of water in the pan?
B. What will happen if all the wood blocks are withdrawn from the plastic cup?

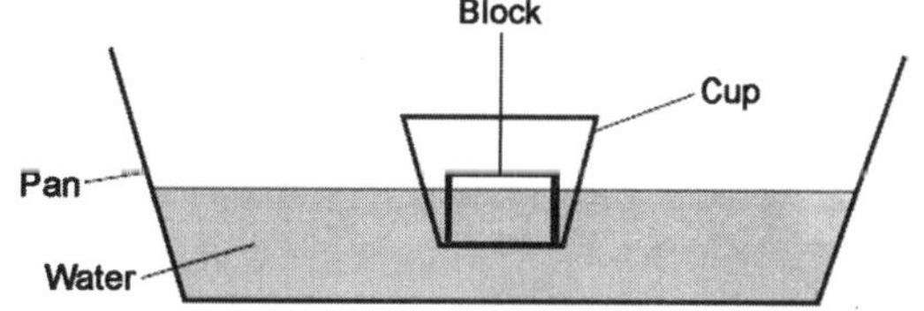

	A	B
(A)	It will go down	The plastic cup will stop floating
(B)	It will go up	The water level will go down
(C)	It will stay the same	
(D)	It will go up and may fill the plastic cup	The water level will go down and empty cup will float on the surface

29. Titanic was one of the largest and luxurious ships that was called THE UNSINKABLE SHIP. On April 14, 1912, however the ship struck an iceberg and early the next day it sank. Some 1500 people perished.
A: The ship sank.

B: The ship got pierced from one corner after hitting the iceberg and the water from the ocean started entering the ship.

C: Ship was floating on the ocean.

D: The fast moving ship hit an iceberg.

Arrange the events in the order in which they took place.

(A) ABDC (B) CDBA

(C) ACDB (D) BACD

30. The pie chart below shows the sources of irrigation of a small district Anantapur which is the second largest source?

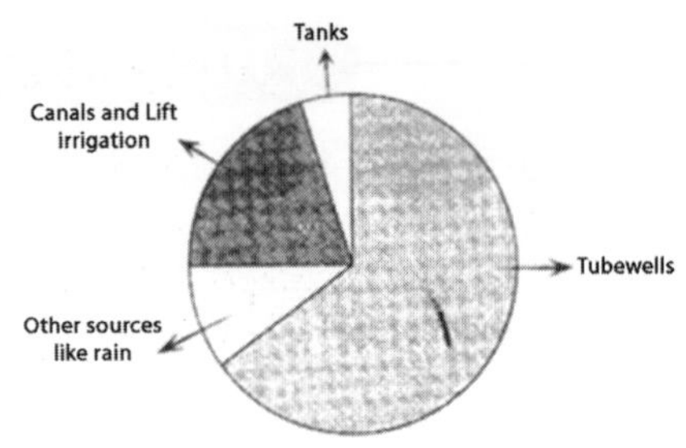

(A) Tanks

(B) Other sources like rain

(C) Tube wells

(D) Canals and lift irrigation

Darken Your Choice with HB Pencil

1.	Ⓐ	Ⓑ	Ⓒ	Ⓓ	7.	Ⓐ	Ⓑ	Ⓒ	Ⓓ	13.	Ⓐ	Ⓑ	Ⓒ	Ⓓ	19	Ⓐ	Ⓑ	Ⓒ	Ⓓ	25.	Ⓐ	Ⓑ	Ⓒ	Ⓓ
2.	Ⓐ	Ⓑ	Ⓒ	Ⓓ	8.	Ⓐ	Ⓑ	Ⓒ	Ⓓ	14.	Ⓐ	Ⓑ	Ⓒ	Ⓓ	20.	Ⓐ	Ⓑ	Ⓒ	Ⓓ	26.	Ⓐ	Ⓑ	Ⓒ	Ⓓ
3.	Ⓐ	Ⓑ	Ⓒ	Ⓓ	9.	Ⓐ	Ⓑ	Ⓒ	Ⓓ	15.	Ⓐ	Ⓑ	Ⓒ	Ⓓ	21.	Ⓐ	Ⓑ	Ⓒ	Ⓓ	27.	Ⓐ	Ⓑ	Ⓒ	Ⓓ
4.	Ⓐ	Ⓑ	Ⓒ	Ⓓ	10.	Ⓐ	Ⓑ	Ⓒ	Ⓓ	16.	Ⓐ	Ⓑ	Ⓒ	Ⓓ	22.	Ⓐ	Ⓑ	Ⓒ	Ⓓ	28.	Ⓐ	Ⓑ	Ⓒ	Ⓓ
5.	Ⓐ	Ⓑ	Ⓒ	Ⓓ	11.	Ⓐ	Ⓑ	Ⓒ	Ⓓ	17.	Ⓐ	Ⓑ	Ⓒ	Ⓓ	23.	Ⓐ	Ⓑ	Ⓒ	Ⓓ	29.	Ⓐ	Ⓑ	Ⓒ	Ⓓ
6.	Ⓐ	Ⓑ	Ⓒ	Ⓓ	12.	Ⓐ	Ⓑ	Ⓒ	Ⓓ	18.	Ⓐ	Ⓑ	Ⓒ	Ⓓ	24.	Ⓐ	Ⓑ	Ⓒ	Ⓓ	30.	Ⓐ	Ⓑ	Ⓒ	Ⓓ

EARTH AND UNIVERSE

LEARNING OBJECTIVES

- Different components of the earth
- Effects of the moon on the earth
- Movement of moon
- Artificial satellites

MULTIPLE CHOICE QUESTIONS

Direction: Select the correct option.

1. There are eight planets in our universe. Say O, P, Q, R, S, T, U, and V. 'S', among all, called the red planet because its soil and rocks are red in colours. This planet resembles Earth the most. Scientists believe that it is the only planet, besides Earth, where life may exist.

   'S' in the above paragraph is ________.

   (A) Venus (B) Mars
   (C) Jupiter (D) Saturn

2. All planets are named in Roman because ________.

   (A) A group of Roman people discovered them.
   (B) They were named by chance in Roman.
   (C) They sound good in Roman.
   (D) None of these

3. Which is the nearest planet to the Sun?

   (A) Jupiter (B) Mercury
   (C) Venus (D) Earth

4. Which is the closest planet to the Earth?

   (A) Jupiter (B) Mercury
   (C) Venus (D) Saturn

5. Which eclipse do you experience if you are standing in the Moon's umbra?

   (A) Partial solar
   (B) Partial lunar
   (C) Total lunar
   (D) Total solar

6. It takes about ________ days for the Moon to complete its cycle of phases.

   (A) 27.5 (B) 28.5
   (C) 29.5 (D) 30.5

7. It takes about ________ days for the Moon to revolve around the Earth.

   (A) 27.5 (B) 27.3
   (C) 29.3 (D) 30.3

8. Which is a group of constellation through which the Sun appears to move?

   (A) Zodiacal (B) Ecliptic
   (C) Equinox (D) Solstice

9. Which movement causes the lunar phases?

   (A) Earth's rotation
   (B) Moon's revolution
   (C) Moon's rotation
   (D) Earth's revolution

10. Which of these planets has the highest gravitational pull?
    (A) Venus
    (B) Mercury
    (C) Jupiter
    (D) Earth
11. Where is the Moon's crust the thinnest?
    (A) On the side farthest to the Earth
    (B) On the side nearest to the Earth
    (C) On the side nearest to the Sun
    (D) On the side farthest to the Sun
12. If the Earth is 93 million miles away from the sun.

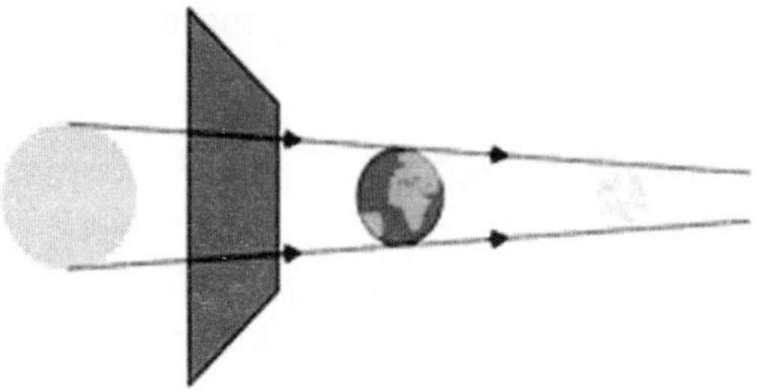

Jupiter is 483.4 million miles away from the sun.

How many miles apart are Jupiter and the Earth from each other?
    (A) 576.4 (B) 393.4
    (C) 390.4 (D) 393
13. A comet is ________.
    (A) A huge group of stars.
    (B) A dirty snowball orbiting the Sun.
    (C) The third planet from the Sun.
    (D) The largest planet in the solar system.
14. What is a constellation?
    (A) A group of planets that form a connect-the-dot type of picture.
    (B) A group of moons that form a connect-the-dot type of picture.
    (C) A group of comets that form a connect-the-dot type of picture.
    (D) A group of stars that form a connect-the-dot type of picture.
15. Gemini, the Twins is the name of ________.
    (A) A planet
    (B) A constellation
    (C) A group of stars
    (D) Both (B) and (C)
16. Earth is closest to the Sun during which season in the northern hemisphere?
    (A) Fall (B) Spring
    (C) Winter (D) Summer
17. Where is the Earth's circumference the greatest?
    (A) Equator (B) Poles
    (C) Mantle (D) Axis
18. We see astronauts floating in space due to the ________.
    (A) Lack of air
    (B) Lack of sound
    (C) Lack of life
    (D) Lack of gravity
19. When the Moon is partly hidden by the dark shadow of the Earth, it is called ________.
    (A) A partial lunar eclipse
    (B) A partial solar eclipse
    (C) A full lunar eclipse
    (D) A full solar eclipse
20. A new moon occurs when the ________.
    (A) Sun is between the Earth and the Moon.
    (B) Moon is between the Earth and the Sun.
    (C) Earth is between the Moon and the Sun.
    (D) None of these
21. An artificial satellite revolves around the Earth in ________.
    (A) An unknown direction
    (B) A fixed direction
    (C) An infinite direction
    (D) A straight direction

22. Which is the first Indian satellite to go into space?
(A) Apollo (B) Aryabhatta
(C) Telstar (D) EDUSAT

23. ________ objects cast shadows.
(A) Transparent
(B) Translucent
(C) Opaque
(D) Both (A) and (C)

24. Which of the following statements are correct?
i. Satellites are small heavenly bodies that revolve around the Sun.
ii. Milky Way is a spiral-shaped galaxy.
iii. Planet Venus has 63 moons.
iv. One revolution of the Earth is complete when it revolves around the Sun, for 365 days.
(A) i and ii
(B) i and iv
(C) ii and iv
(D) iii and iv

25. The first American satellite was named as ________ and it was put into orbit on ________.
(A) Navigator - 1, Jan 30, 1958
(B) Navigator - A, Feb 28, 1968
(C) Explorer - 1, Jan 31, 1958
(D) Explorer - A, Jan 30, 1968

HOTS (ACHIEVERS SECTION)

26. Sumit built this model of the Sun, the Moon, and the Earth.

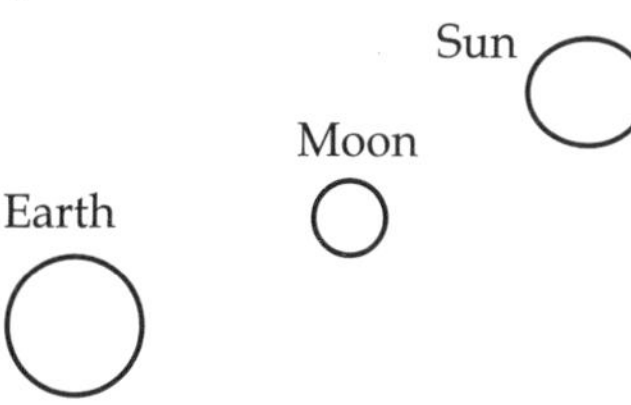

A. Which phase of the Moon is shown in Sumit's model?
B. Where will the moon enter to cause total lunar eclipse?

	A	B
(A)	Full moon	Umbra
(B)	New moon	Penumbra
(C)	Full moon	Penumbra
(D)	Third quarter	Umbra

27. Which of the senses must be protected when doing an activity concerning a solar eclipse?
I. Touch
II. Taste
III. Sight
IV. Smell
(A) I and II
(B) I and III
(C) III and IV
(D) I and IV

28. Ayush was born in May 2000. When would Ayush see the next Halley's comet if last time it was seen in 1986?
(A) 2050
(B) 2063
(C) 2062
(D) 2060

29. Anil draws the diagrams of the moon he sees one night (A) and after a few nights (B). Why does the moon look different at different nights?

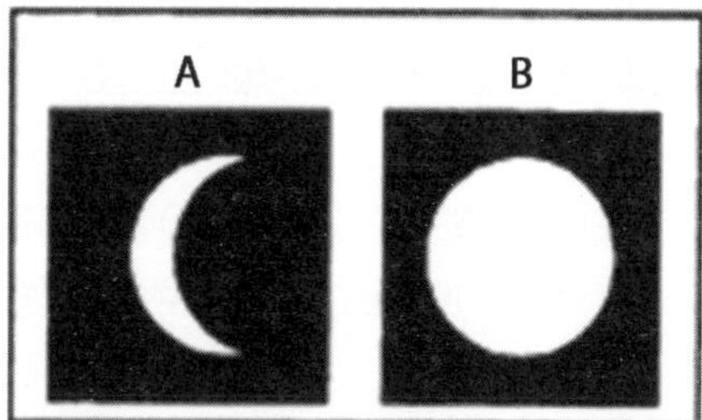

(A) Revolution of the moon around the earth.
(B) Rotation of the moon.
(C) Revolution of the moon around the sun.
(D) Both (A) and (C)

30. What are the areas where satellites can be used?
(i) Weather forecasts
(ii) Telecommunications
(iii) Data transmission
(A) Only (i) and (ii)
(B) Only (i) and (iii)
(C) Only (ii) and (iii)
(D) (i), (ii) and (iii)

Darken Your Choice with HB Pencil

1.	Ⓐ	Ⓑ	Ⓒ	Ⓓ	7.	Ⓐ	Ⓑ	Ⓒ	Ⓓ	13.	Ⓐ	Ⓑ	Ⓒ	Ⓓ	19	Ⓐ	Ⓑ	Ⓒ	Ⓓ	25.	Ⓐ	Ⓑ	Ⓒ	Ⓓ
2.	Ⓐ	Ⓑ	Ⓒ	Ⓓ	8.	Ⓐ	Ⓑ	Ⓒ	Ⓓ	14.	Ⓐ	Ⓑ	Ⓒ	Ⓓ	20.	Ⓐ	Ⓑ	Ⓒ	Ⓓ	26.	Ⓐ	Ⓑ	Ⓒ	Ⓓ
3.	Ⓐ	Ⓑ	Ⓒ	Ⓓ	9.	Ⓐ	Ⓑ	Ⓒ	Ⓓ	15.	Ⓐ	Ⓑ	Ⓒ	Ⓓ	21.	Ⓐ	Ⓑ	Ⓒ	Ⓓ	27.	Ⓐ	Ⓑ	Ⓒ	Ⓓ
4.	Ⓐ	Ⓑ	Ⓒ	Ⓓ	10.	Ⓐ	Ⓑ	Ⓒ	Ⓓ	16.	Ⓐ	Ⓑ	Ⓒ	Ⓓ	22.	Ⓐ	Ⓑ	Ⓒ	Ⓓ	28.	Ⓐ	Ⓑ	Ⓒ	Ⓓ
5.	Ⓐ	Ⓑ	Ⓒ	Ⓓ	11.	Ⓐ	Ⓑ	Ⓒ	Ⓓ	17.	Ⓐ	Ⓑ	Ⓒ	Ⓓ	23.	Ⓐ	Ⓑ	Ⓒ	Ⓓ	29.	Ⓐ	Ⓑ	Ⓒ	Ⓓ
6.	Ⓐ	Ⓑ	Ⓒ	Ⓓ	12.	Ⓐ	Ⓑ	Ⓒ	Ⓓ	18.	Ⓐ	Ⓑ	Ⓒ	Ⓓ	24.	Ⓐ	Ⓑ	Ⓒ	Ⓓ	30.	Ⓐ	Ⓑ	Ⓒ	Ⓓ

MATTER AND MATERIALS

LEARNING OBJECTIVES

- Classification of matter
- Effect of temperature in inter-conversion of matter
- Conservation of matter

MULTIPLE CHOICE QUESTIONS

Direction: Select the correct option.

1. Intermolecular space is very weak between ______.
   (A) Gas molecules
   (B) Solid molecules
   (C) Liquid molecules
   (D) Both (A) and (B)
2. Intermolecular force is very strong between ______.
   (A) Gas molecules
   (B) Solid molecules
   (C) Liquid molecules
   (D) Both (A) and (B)

Direction (3 – 4): Four thin sheets of material P, Q, R, and S of similar sizes were weighed individually. Then they were put into four beakers containing equal amounts of water. After 15 minutes, each sheet was weighed again. Their masses were recorded in the table below.

Material	Mass at the Beginning	Mass after 15 minutes
P	10 g	20 g
Q	12 g	12 g
R	14 g	16 g
S	14 g	20 g

3. Which material absorbs the most amount of water?
   (A) P (B) Q
   (C) R (D) S
4. Which material will be the most suitable for making a tent?
   (A) P (B) Q
   (C) R (D) S
5. 0°C: Freezing point of water
   ______: Boiling point of water
   (A) 110°C (B) 100°C
   (C) 120°C (D) 98°C
6. A substance changes from a solid to a liquid. Which point has it reached?
   (A) Boiling (B) Melting
   (C) Freezing (D) Sublimation
7. Which of the following is true for the molecules of gases?
   (A) They can move around freely.
   (B) They have a fixed volume.
   (C) They have a fixed shape.
   (D) They cannot move freely.

8. When heat is supplied to molecules, their _________ energy increases.
(A) Chemical
(B) Kinetic
(C) Potential
(D) Electrical

9. Pick the correct option.
(A) Solids can freeze
(B) Liquids can freeze
(C) Gases can freeze
(D) All of these

10. Molecules are the components of _________.
(A) Solids
(B) Matter
(C) Solutions
(D) All of these

11. Heat is a form of _________.
(A) Work
(B) Machine
(C) Energy
(D) Force

12. Which of the following is not a form of energy?
(A) Light
(B) Electricity
(C) Heat
(D) Temperature

13. Husk can be removed from the grain by _________.
(A) Winnowing
(B) Handpicking
(C) Evaporation
(D) Magnetic separation

14. Diwali is a famous festival of India. In this festival people burn crackers. When these crackers burn, they turn into ashes. What is such burning of crackers an example of?
(A) Chemical change
(B) Physical change
(C) Both physical and chemical change
(D) None of these

15. Matter is made up of these particles _________.
(A) Bubbles
(B) Molecules
(C) Atoms
(D) Circles

16. Melting is the opposite of _________.
(A) Vapourization
(B) Freezing
(C) Sublimation
(D) Condensation

17. The difference between boiling and evaporation is _________.
(A) Evaporation occurs at one temperature only while boiling may occur at different temperatures.
(B) Boiling changes the liquid into a gas while evaporation makes the liquid disappear.
(C) Boiling occurs at one temperature while evaporation may occur at different temperatures.
(D) There is no difference between boiling and evaporation as in each case a liquid is changed into a gas.

18. Two substances, P and Q, were used to fill a syringe. The plunger was then pushed in as shown in the diagram. Which of the following would most likely be P and which would be Q?

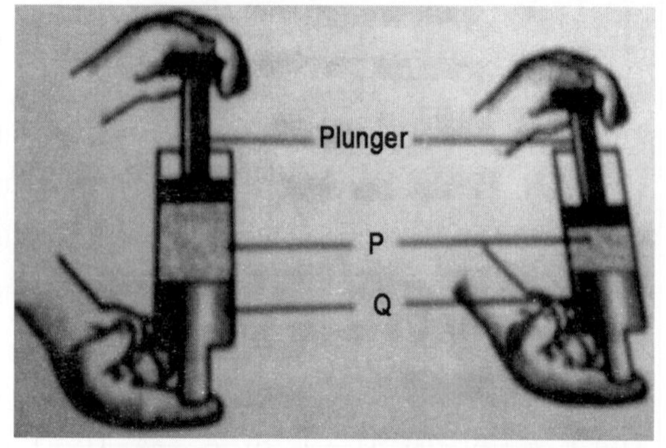

P	Q
(A) Oil	Salt
(B) Rice	Oxygen
(C) Air	Water
(D) Flour	Water vapour

19. Gases consist of particles that ________.
    (A) Are packed close together
    (B) Are strongly attracted to each other
    (C) Have a regular arrangement
    (D) Are very far apart

20. Which change of state occurs when particles in a solid begin to move slowly past each other?

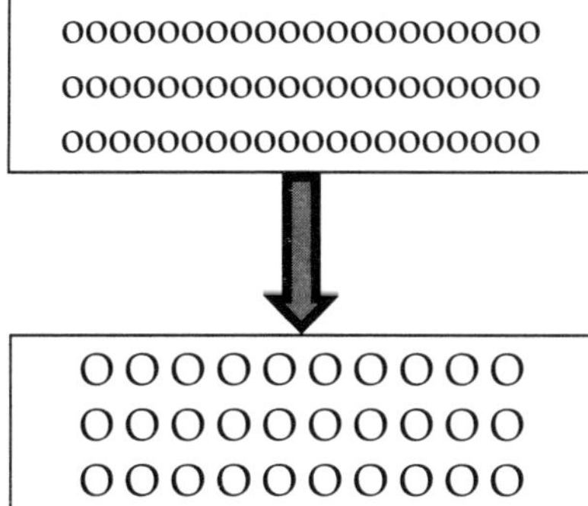

    (A) Subliming
    (B) Melting
    (C) Freezing
    (D) Boiling

21. There is a gold chain weighing 100 g. If the jeweller melts 100 g of pure gold and sells it, he will get ________.
    (A) Price for 100 g of gold
    (B) Price for 80 g of gold
    (C) Price for 130 g of gold
    (D) Price for 10 g of gold

22. Which of the following is a physical change?
    (A) Changing of wheat to bread
    (B) Rusting of iron
    (C) Melting of butter
    (D) Burning of paper

23. What determines the speed of the atoms and molecules of a particular substance?
    (A) Size of the atoms and molecules
    (B) Temperature of the substance
    (C) Both (A) and (B)
    (D) None of these

24. When ice melts to form water, energy ________.
    (A) Is created
    (B) Is released
    (C) Is destroyed
    (D) Is absorbed

25. The ability to change or to move matter is referred to as ________.
    (A) Kinetic theory
    (B) Energy
    (C) Evaporation
    (D) Heating

26. As the temperature of a fixed amount of gas at constant volume decreases, its pressure ________.
    (A) Increases
    (B) Decreases
    (C) Stay the same
    (D) None of these

27. As the volume of a fixed amount of gas at constant temperature decreases, its pressure ________.
    (A) Increases
    (B) Decreases
    (C) Stay the same
    (D) None of these

28. Mist seen often around ice cubes. Which of the following is a probable reason?
    (A) Water molecules in the ice vapourize.
    (B) Water vapour in air condenses when they hit the ice surface.
    (C) The ice cools the air around it, thus producing a visible convection current.
    (D) The air molecule gets cold and become denser around ice cubes.

29. Which state of matter has particles able to slide past each other, yet still packed together?
(A) Solids (B) Liquids
(C) Gases (D) None of these

30. The most common state of matter in the universe is called ________.
(A) Solid (B) Liquid
(C) Gas (D) Plasma

HOTS (ACHIEVERS SECTION)

31. Read the following.
Liquid:
(i) Flow and fill the shape of the container up to a definite volume.
(ii) Move quickly and fill any available space.
(iii) Tightly packed and keep their shape.
Gases:
(i) Gases have a definite volume, but solids and liquids do not.
(ii) Gases and liquids have no definite volume, but solids do.
(iii) Gases and liquids have a definite volume, but solids do not.
(iv) Gases gave no definite volume, but solids and liquids do.
Which two questions you can extract from above description?
(A) How are liquids different from solids? How are gases different from solids and liquids?
(B) How are gases different from solids and liquids? How are liquids different from solids?
(C) Why are liquids and solids different from each other?
(D) Differentiate between solids, liquids, and gases.

32. A pencil is lying in front of you. How many different types of matter are used to make it?

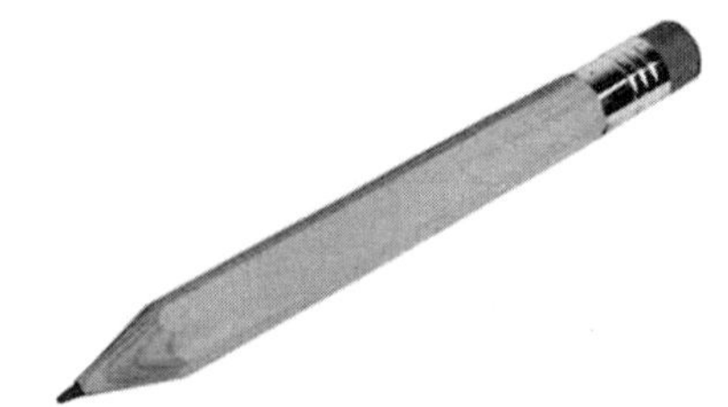

(A) Rubber, wood, graphite and clay
(B) Rubber, metal, graphite and clay
(C) Rubber, metal, wood, graphite and clay
(D) Rubber, metal and wood

33. Water present in container 'P' is transferred to container 'Q' as shown in the figure. Which of the following will undergo a change because of the transfer?

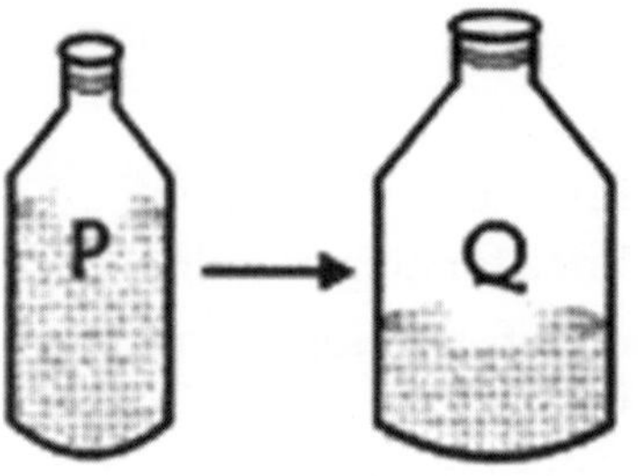

(A) Volume (B) Mass
(C) Temperature (D) Shape

34. When we heat a substance in solid form, it becomes liquid and then into gas. This shows that by heating, the space occupied by the substance generally:
(A) Increases
(B) decrease
(C) Remains same
(D) changes minutely

35. In the table given below, states of matter, their properties and examples are represented by letters W, X, Y, Z.

State of matter	Properties	Example
W	Has a definite shape	Book
Liquid	X	Petrol
Y	Has no definite volume or shape	Z

Carbon dioxide can be placed in the place of letter________.
(A) X (B) Y
(C) Z (D) W

Darken Your Choice with HB Pencil

1.	Ⓐ Ⓑ Ⓒ Ⓓ	8.	Ⓐ Ⓑ Ⓒ Ⓓ	15.	Ⓐ Ⓑ Ⓒ Ⓓ	22	Ⓐ Ⓑ Ⓒ Ⓓ	29.	Ⓐ Ⓑ Ⓒ Ⓓ
2.	Ⓐ Ⓑ Ⓒ Ⓓ	9.	Ⓐ Ⓑ Ⓒ Ⓓ	16.	Ⓐ Ⓑ Ⓒ Ⓓ	23.	Ⓐ Ⓑ Ⓒ Ⓓ	30.	Ⓐ Ⓑ Ⓒ Ⓓ
3.	Ⓐ Ⓑ Ⓒ Ⓓ	10.	Ⓐ Ⓑ Ⓒ Ⓓ	17.	Ⓐ Ⓑ Ⓒ Ⓓ	24.	Ⓐ Ⓑ Ⓒ Ⓓ	31.	Ⓐ Ⓑ Ⓒ Ⓓ
4.	Ⓐ Ⓑ Ⓒ Ⓓ	11.	Ⓐ Ⓑ Ⓒ Ⓓ	18.	Ⓐ Ⓑ Ⓒ Ⓓ	25.	Ⓐ Ⓑ Ⓒ Ⓓ	32.	Ⓐ Ⓑ Ⓒ Ⓓ
5.	Ⓐ Ⓑ Ⓒ Ⓓ	12.	Ⓐ Ⓑ Ⓒ Ⓓ	19.	Ⓐ Ⓑ Ⓒ Ⓓ	26.	Ⓐ Ⓑ Ⓒ Ⓓ	33.	Ⓐ Ⓑ Ⓒ Ⓓ
6.	Ⓐ Ⓑ Ⓒ Ⓓ	13.	Ⓐ Ⓑ Ⓒ Ⓓ	20.	Ⓐ Ⓑ Ⓒ Ⓓ	27.	Ⓐ Ⓑ Ⓒ Ⓓ	34.	Ⓐ Ⓑ Ⓒ Ⓓ
7.	Ⓐ Ⓑ Ⓒ Ⓓ	14.	Ⓐ Ⓑ Ⓒ Ⓓ	21.	Ⓐ Ⓑ Ⓒ Ⓓ	28.	Ⓐ Ⓑ Ⓒ Ⓓ	35.	Ⓐ Ⓑ Ⓒ Ⓓ

FORCE, WORK AND ENERGY

LEARNING OBJECTIVES

- Types of force
- Work
- Conservation of energy and transformation of energy

MULTIPLE CHOICE QUESTIONS

Direction: Select the correct option.

1. Change in the state of rest of uniform motion is brought about by ________.
   (A) Energy (B) Force
   (C) Acceleration (D) None of these
2. Friction force always opposes ________.
   (A) The state of rest
   (B) The state of rest and motion
   (C) The state of motion
   (D) None of these
3. We do sprinkle powder before playing carrom. Why?
   (A) To decrease friction
   (B) To increase friction
   (C) Depending on the type of game, to increase or decrease the friction
   (D) None of these
4. When the load is nearer the fulcrum than the effort, it is ________.
   (A) Easier to move
   (B) Difficult to move
   (C) Moves faster
   (D) Both (A) and (C)
5. When the load is further from the fulcrum than the effort, it ________.
   (A) Moves slower
   (B) Moves faster
   (C) Easier to move
   (D) Difficult to move
6. You have just kicked a ball, and it is now sliding across the ground, about 2 meters in front of you. Which of these forces act on the ball?
   (A) Gravity, acting downward
   (B) The normal force, acting upward
   (C) Friction, acting opposite the direction of motion
   (D) All of these
7. Two rubber bands stretched the standard distance cause an object to accelerate at 2 m/s^2. Suppose another object with twice the mass is pulled by four rubber bands stretched the standard length. The acceleration of this second object is ________.
   (A) 16 m/s^2 (B) 8 m/s^2
   (C) 4 m/s^2 (D) 2 m/s^2

8. Three forces act on an object. In which direction does the object accelerate?

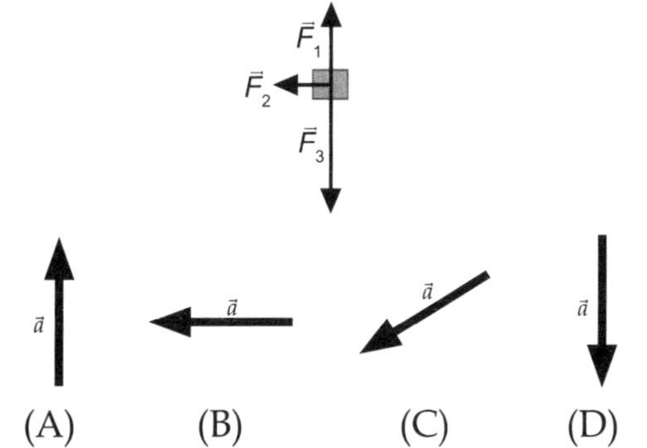

9. A simple machine ________.
   (A) Is used to make work easier
   (B) Has an engine
   (C) Is simple because it is easy to use
   (D) Is not actually simple to use

10. To press or fasten objects like the book binding press, is an example of ________.
   (A) Pulley
   (B) Wedge
   (C) Screw
   (D) Lever

11. Levers are simple machines which have ________.
   (A) Fulcrum and a stone
   (B) A rod and a fulcrum
   (C) A stone and an iron rod
   (D) Can be all of these

12. What type of simple machine is found on the floor of a bath tub?
   (A) Screw
   (B) Inclined plane
   (C) Wedge
   (D) Pulley

13. Which of these is an example of a wedge?
   (A) Skateboard
   (B) Butter knife
   (C) Broom
   (D) Stairs

14. A screw is made up of ________ wrapped around a post or rod.
   (A) Treads (B) Springs
   (C) Threads (D) Strings

15. Which of these is not an example of an inclined plane?
   (A) Stairs (B) Wall
   (C) Driveway (D) Ladder

16. Pulley is mainly used to lift objects above the ground, thus this opposes ________.
   (A) Gravitational force
   (B) Muscular force
   (C) Frictional force
   (D) Tension force

17. Gravity is defined as ________.
   (A) The pull of the Earth
   (B) The push of the Earth
   (C) The force of the Earth
   (D) The capacity of the Earth

18. Fulcrum of lever acts as a ________.
   (A) Support
   (B) Burden
   (C) Additional weight
   (D) An iron rod

19. Bicycle is an example of ________.
   (A) Pulley
   (B) Simple machine
   (C) Wedge
   (D) Compound machine

20. Radio converts ________.
   (A) Electric energy into heat energy
   (B) Electric energy into sound energy
   (C) Mechanical energy into electric energy
   (D) Solar energy into electrical energy

21. Which form of energy would move a cart?
   (A) Heat energy
   (B) Electrical energy
   (C) Solar energy
   (D) Mechanical energy

22. Energy can't be created or destroyed, it can only be changed from one type into another type. We call this rule ________.
   (A) Conversion of energy
   (B) Loss of energy
   (C) Conservation of energy
   (D) None of these

23. Imagine a brick falling from a wall. The brick originally has only potential energy. As the brick falls, it loses potential energy but gains kinetic energy. This is due to ________.
   (A) Conservation of energy
   (B) Loss of energy
   (C) Conversion of energy
   (D) Both (A) and (C)

24. How do we calculate the work done?
   (A) Energy transformed = work done = applied force × distance
   (B) Energy transformed = applied force = work done × distance
   (C) Energy transformed = distance = work done × applied force
   (D) Energy transformed = work done × distance

25. If an object does not move when force is applied then ________.
   (A) Appropriate force is not applied
   (B) Object needs more force to move
   (C) No work is done
   (D) All of these

26. Choose the correct statement.
   (A) Energy is the ability to do work and is used in order to perform work.
   (B) Energy is the rate at which work is done.
   (C) There are various units of energy, work, and energy.
   (D) All of these

27. What is the definition of energy?
   (A) The capacity for work
   (B) Energy is the ability to make something happen
   (C) Both (A) and (B)
   (D) None of these

28. Musical instruments and traffic on road are examples of ________.
   (A) Sound energy
   (B) Heat energy
   (C) Solar energy
   (D) Mechanical energy

29. A river possesses ______ as a result of the movement of water.
   (A) Mechanical energy
   (B) Chemical energy
   (C) Electrical energy
   (D) Kinetic energy

30. ______ is based on mechanical energy.
   (A) Electronic press
   (B) Tube light
   (C) LPG
   (D) Washing machine

31. Look at the image of the pulley.

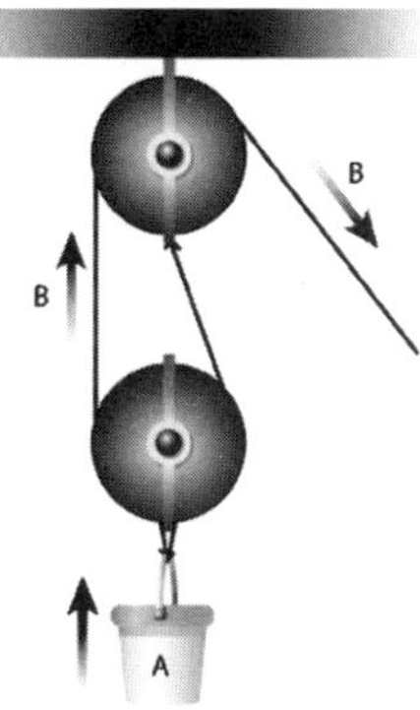

Read the following table carefully and find out the correct option.

Bucket weight	Minimum effort/Force required to lift the bucket
I. 5 kgs.	It would take 0 kg of effort to lift the bucket
II. 5 kgs.	It would take 2.5 kg of effort to lift the bucket, if friction is ignored.
III. 10 kgs.	It would take 5 kg of effort to lift the bucket, if friction is ignored.
IV. 10 kgs.	It would take 0 kg of effort to lift the bucket, if friction is ignored.

(A) I and IV (B) II and IV
(C) II and III (D) III

32. Identify the image. It is an example of which type of simple machine?

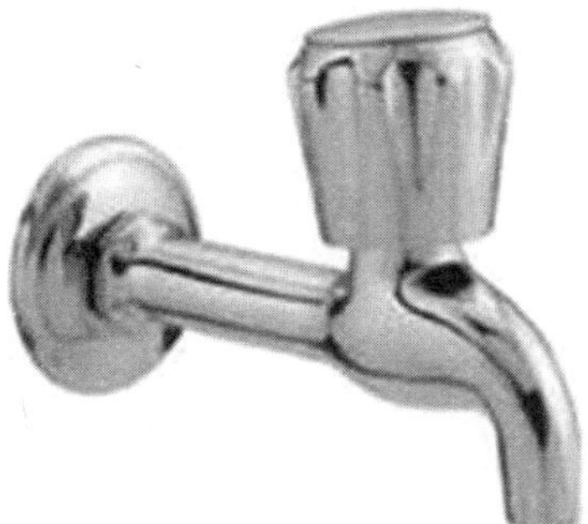

Instrument	Type of Simple Machine
I. Faucet handle	Wheel and axle
II. Shower	Wheel and axle
III. Tap	Pulley
IV. Puller	Second-class lever

(A) I and II (B) I
(C) II and IV (D) I, II, and IV

33. Some students were conducting an experiment at a stream. On the basis of the conclusions, answer the following questions:
   (i) They saw that the larger a rock was, the bigger the splash it made. The students wondered if this was because larger objects fall faster.
   (ii) The next day, the students decided to conduct an experiment in the school yard using an orange, a rock, and a basketball. They asked one of the students to drop the objects from a tall ladder while they wrote down the time it took for each object to reach the ground. The table below shows the data the students collected.

Object	Object weight (grams)	Time taken to fall to the ground (seconds)
Rock	1250	2
Orange	150	5
Basketball	900	3

Using the above information, choose the correct option (if air friction is ignored).
(A) Weight and size both affect the time it takes an object to fall to the ground.

(B) Only the weight of an object affects the time it takes an object to fall to the ground.
(C) Weight and size of the object has no effect on the time it takes an object to fall to the ground.
(D) Only the size of an object affects the time it takes an object to fall to the ground.

34. Rocks in the stream that the students were studying were smoother than the rocks found on the shore of the stream. What could be the possible reason for this?
(A) Fishes make the rocks smooth.
(B) Continuous collision of rocks among each other due to movement of water made them smooth.
(C) The falling of rocks in the river bed makes them smooth.
(D) Only smooth rocks fall in the river.

35. The table given below is incomplete. Which tools would you add in the table to complete it?

distance, length, or height	meter stick or tape measure
mass and weight	balance or scale
volume	beaker or graduated cylinder
temperature	thermometer
time	watch, clock

(A) Ruler, stopwatch, weighing machine
(B) Stopwatch
(C) Compass
(D) Ruler

Darken Your Choice with HB Pencil

1.	Ⓐ Ⓑ Ⓒ Ⓓ	8.	Ⓐ Ⓑ Ⓒ Ⓓ	15.	Ⓐ Ⓑ Ⓒ Ⓓ	22	Ⓐ Ⓑ Ⓒ Ⓓ	29.	Ⓐ Ⓑ Ⓒ Ⓓ
2.	Ⓐ Ⓑ Ⓒ Ⓓ	9.	Ⓐ Ⓑ Ⓒ Ⓓ	16.	Ⓐ Ⓑ Ⓒ Ⓓ	23.	Ⓐ Ⓑ Ⓒ Ⓓ	30.	Ⓐ Ⓑ Ⓒ Ⓓ
3.	Ⓐ Ⓑ Ⓒ Ⓓ	10.	Ⓐ Ⓑ Ⓒ Ⓓ	17.	Ⓐ Ⓑ Ⓒ Ⓓ	24.	Ⓐ Ⓑ Ⓒ Ⓓ	31.	Ⓐ Ⓑ Ⓒ Ⓓ
4.	Ⓐ Ⓑ Ⓒ Ⓓ	11.	Ⓐ Ⓑ Ⓒ Ⓓ	18.	Ⓐ Ⓑ Ⓒ Ⓓ	25.	Ⓐ Ⓑ Ⓒ Ⓓ	32.	Ⓐ Ⓑ Ⓒ Ⓓ
5.	Ⓐ Ⓑ Ⓒ Ⓓ	12.	Ⓐ Ⓑ Ⓒ Ⓓ	19.	Ⓐ Ⓑ Ⓒ Ⓓ	26.	Ⓐ Ⓑ Ⓒ Ⓓ	33.	Ⓐ Ⓑ Ⓒ Ⓓ
6.	Ⓐ Ⓑ Ⓒ Ⓓ	13.	Ⓐ Ⓑ Ⓒ Ⓓ	20.	Ⓐ Ⓑ Ⓒ Ⓓ	27.	Ⓐ Ⓑ Ⓒ Ⓓ	34.	Ⓐ Ⓑ Ⓒ Ⓓ
7.	Ⓐ Ⓑ Ⓒ Ⓓ	14.	Ⓐ Ⓑ Ⓒ Ⓓ	21.	Ⓐ Ⓑ Ⓒ Ⓓ	28.	Ⓐ Ⓑ Ⓒ Ⓓ	35.	Ⓐ Ⓑ Ⓒ Ⓓ

ECOSYSTEM AND GENERAL SCIENCE

LEARNING OBJECTIVES

- ➤ Ecosystem and different types of ecosystem
- ➤ Components of ecosystem
- ➤ Astronomy and earth science

MULTIPLE CHOICE QUESTIONS

Direction: Select the correct option.

1. A plant is ____________.
   (A) An autotroph
   (B) A heterotroph
   (C) A primary produce
   (D) Both (A) and (C)
2. Evergreen forests grow in the high ____________.
   (A) Rainfall areas of the Western Ghats
   (B) Rainfall areas of North Eastern India
   (C) Rainfall areas of Andaman and Nicobar Islands
   (D) All of these
3. Plants found in which of the following habitats have a poorly developed root system?
   (A) Aquatic (B) Terrestrial
   (C) Xerophytic (D) Amphibious
4. The largest unit of the biological system is ____________.
   (A) Population (B) Biome
   (C) Biosphere (D) Ecosystem
5. The apex position in the pyramid of numbers is occupied by ____________.
   (A) Producers
   (B) Small carnivores
   (C) Large carnivores
   (D) Herbivores
6. Nutrients present in plants and animals are used again and again with the help of ____________.
   (A) Consumers (B) Decomposers
   (C) Producers (D) Herbivores
7. Study the following chain. Who among the following can be termed as consumers?
   Plants → Rabbit → Snake → Eagle
   (A) Rabbit
   (B) Plants
   (C) Rabbit, Snake, Eagle
   (D) Eagle
8. When we destroy a forest, we destroy ____________.
   (A) An ecosystem
   (B) A Biome
   (C) A population
   (D) Wild animals
9. Pesticides sprayed on the crop can ____________.

(A) Enter the food chain
(B) Destroy useful insects
(C) (A), (B), and (C)
(D) Enhance crop health

10. Which of the following set represents primary consumers?
(A) Cows and giraffes
(B) Buffaloes and cats
(C) Insects and butterflies
(D) All of these

11. Which of the following is a biotic factor?
(A) Light (B) Air
(C) Soil (D) Saprophyte

12. The number of links in a food chain ________.
(A) 0 (B) 1
(C) 2 (D) >2

13. The species that is threatened with extinction is called ________.
(A) Endangered species
(B) Rare species
(C) Extinct species
(D) Sensitive species

14. Aquatic microscopic animals are called ________.
(A) Consumers (B) Carnivores
(C) Saprophytes (D) Zooplankton

15. Which of these is a biodegradable waste?
(A) Animal excreta
(B) Vegetable scrap
(C) Paper
(D) All of these

16. Greenhouse effect causes ________.
(A) Melting of ice caps
(B) Rise in the sea level
(C) Submerging of low lying areas
(D) All of these

17. What is true of an ecosystem?
(A) Primary consumers are least dependent upon producers.
(B) Primary consumers outnumber producers.
(C) Producers are more than primary consumers.
(D) Secondary consumers are the largest and most powerful.

18. The sum total of population of the same kind of organisms constitute a ________.
(A) Colony (B) Genus
(C) Species (D) Community

19. ________ is any chemical substance that an organism requires to live.
(A) Carbohydrate
(B) Nutrient
(C) Sunlight
(D) Water

20. The sum total of the variety of organisms in the biosphere is called ________.
(A) A biotic factor
(B) An abiotic factor
(C) Biodiversity
(D) A population

21. The total amount of living tissue within a given trophic level is known as ________.
(A) Biomass
(B) Biosphere
(C) Food chain
(D) Niche

22. The term 'detritivore' includes ________.
(A) Decomposers
(B) Primary consumers
(C) Secondary consumers
(D) Autotrophs

23. Biodiversity is described as ________.
(A) The range of different species in an environment.
(B) The seasonal and daily changes in an environment.
(C) The way species differ from one another.
(D) The influence of physical factors on an environment.

24. Which of these is a correct food chain?
   (A) Fish → Chips → Peas
   (B) Man → Cow → Grass
   (C) Cow → Farm → Supermarket
   (D) Grass → Cow → Man
25. What does a pyramid of biomass represent?
   (A) The energy available at each trophic level.
   (B) The number of organisms at each trophic level.
   (C) The number of food chains at each trophic level.
   (D) The total mass of living things at each trophic level.
26. Bacteria and fungi serve an important role as __________.
   (A) Omnivores (B) Detrivores
   (C) Producers (D) Decomposers
27. The relationship between a human and a tapeworm is __________.
   (A) Commensalism (B) Predation
   (C) Parasitism (D) Mutualism
28. The arrows in a food chain represent __________.
   (A) Who eats whom
   (B) The route of food through the digestive system.
   (C) How food travels
   (D) The movement of energy through different organisms.
29. A fish tank is an ecosystem because it includes __________.
   (A) The living community
   (B) A physical environment
   (C) The living community as well as a physical environment
   (D) None of these
30. ________ feed on the waste material in an ecosystem including animal remains, animal faeces, and plant debris.
   (A) Producers
   (B) Detrivores
   (C) Decomposers
   (D) Both detrivores and decomposers

HOTS (ACHIEVERS SECTION)

31. Neeta, Rohit, Shree, and Shobhit were discussing the definition of ecosystem, community, population, and species. Which of the following definitions is correct?
   (A) Neeta: A community consists of the interaction between groups of different individuals and the non-living factors in a particular area.
   (B) Rohit: A population consists of the interaction between groups of different individuals and the non-living factors in a particular area.
   (C) Shree: An ecosystem consists of the interaction between groups of different individuals and the non-living factors in a particular area.
   (D) Shobhit: A species is a group of different individuals in a particular area.
32. Study the grid below and answer the following questions.

F	T	U	N	D	R	A	V	T	E	V
F	G	H	J	U	I	O	K	M	L	M
R	T	D	G	A	D	I	J	A	C	H
E	H	E	H	Z	E	W	E	R	X	N
S	R	S	J	O	G	Q	W	I	Z	B
H	T	S	N	U	T	Y	J	N	Z	V

W	Q	E	D	J	F	O	R	E	S	T
A	G	R	A	S	S	L	A	N	D	O
T	B	T	E	E	T	A	I	G	A	P
E	N	O	T	H	F	W	L	Y	Q	W
R	S	M	O	U	N	T	A	I	N	M

What are the number of ecosystems in the grid?

(A) Three (B) Seven

(C) Six (D) Five

33. Which biome in the grid has a very cold season throughout the year? The vegetation in this biome mostly includes shrubs, lichens, grasses and mosses.

(A) Desert (B) Taiga

(C) Rainforest (D) Tundra

34. Complete the missing link of the following marine food chain.

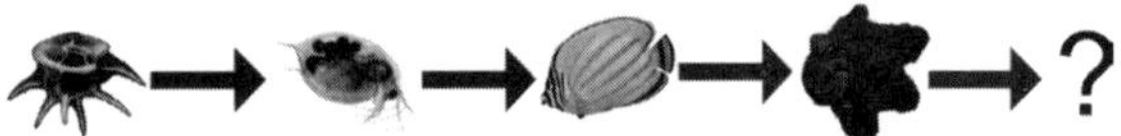

(A) Shark (B) Elephant

(C) Snail (D) Shrimp

35. Match the following:

List I		List II	
A		1	Decomposer
B		2	Producer
C		3	Consumer
D		4	Scavanger

	A	B	C	D
(A)	2	1	3	4
(B)	2	3	4	1
(C)	4	1	3	2
(D)	1	3	2	4

Darken Your Choice with HB Pencil

1.	Ⓐ Ⓑ Ⓒ Ⓓ	8.	Ⓐ Ⓑ Ⓒ Ⓓ	15.	Ⓐ Ⓑ Ⓒ Ⓓ	22	Ⓐ Ⓑ Ⓒ Ⓓ	29.	Ⓐ Ⓑ Ⓒ Ⓓ
2.	Ⓐ Ⓑ Ⓒ Ⓓ	9.	Ⓐ Ⓑ Ⓒ Ⓓ	16.	Ⓐ Ⓑ Ⓒ Ⓓ	23.	Ⓐ Ⓑ Ⓒ Ⓓ	30.	Ⓐ Ⓑ Ⓒ Ⓓ
3.	Ⓐ Ⓑ Ⓒ Ⓓ	10.	Ⓐ Ⓑ Ⓒ Ⓓ	17.	Ⓐ Ⓑ Ⓒ Ⓓ	24.	Ⓐ Ⓑ Ⓒ Ⓓ	31.	Ⓐ Ⓑ Ⓒ Ⓓ
4.	Ⓐ Ⓑ Ⓒ Ⓓ	11.	Ⓐ Ⓑ Ⓒ Ⓓ	18.	Ⓐ Ⓑ Ⓒ Ⓓ	25.	Ⓐ Ⓑ Ⓒ Ⓓ	32.	Ⓐ Ⓑ Ⓒ Ⓓ
5.	Ⓐ Ⓑ Ⓒ Ⓓ	12.	Ⓐ Ⓑ Ⓒ Ⓓ	19.	Ⓐ Ⓑ Ⓒ Ⓓ	26.	Ⓐ Ⓑ Ⓒ Ⓓ	33.	Ⓐ Ⓑ Ⓒ Ⓓ
6.	Ⓐ Ⓑ Ⓒ Ⓓ	13.	Ⓐ Ⓑ Ⓒ Ⓓ	20.	Ⓐ Ⓑ Ⓒ Ⓓ	27.	Ⓐ Ⓑ Ⓒ Ⓓ	34.	Ⓐ Ⓑ Ⓒ Ⓓ
7.	Ⓐ Ⓑ Ⓒ Ⓓ	14.	Ⓐ Ⓑ Ⓒ Ⓓ	21.	Ⓐ Ⓑ Ⓒ Ⓓ	28.	Ⓐ Ⓑ Ⓒ Ⓓ	35.	Ⓐ Ⓑ Ⓒ Ⓓ

LOGICAL REASONING

LEARNING OBJECTIVES

- The missing term
- Asymmetrical letter/number
- Types of analogy
- Various objects, words and letters based on their common characterstics
- Rules of coding and decoding
- Different types of coding and decoding
- Direction and displacement
- Positions of objects
- Arranging objects in different ranks
- Arranging alphabets
- Logical sequence of words
- Puzzles based on the logic
- Reflection of an object or a person in mirror
- Reflection of images in water
- Embedded figure
- Various geometrical shapes

MULTIPLE CHOICE QUESTIONS

Directions (1–5): In each of the following questions, missing terms are shown by (?). Choose the missing term from the given alternatives.

1. D F I M ?

(A) P (B) Q
(C) R (D) T

2. PZA QYC RXE SWG ?

(A) TVB (B) TVI
(C) TVG (D) TVP

3. K5M I8P G11S E14V ?

(A) C17Y (B) C15X
(C) B17Z (D) B17W

4. AEI BFJ CGK ?

(A) DGK (B) DHK
(C) DHI (D) DHL

5. 36 34 30 28 24 ?

(A) 22 (B) 24
(C) 25 (D) 23

6. 'Gun' is related to 'Bullet', in the same way as 'Bow' is related to ____________.

(A) Arrow (B) String
(C) Bamboo (D) Archery

7. As 'Bald' is related to 'Blond', in the same way as 'Barren' is related to _________.

(A) Farm (B) Fertile
(C) Vegetation (D) Inhibited

8. 'Disease' is related to 'Medicine', in the same way as Famine is related to ____________.

(A) Drought (B) Waterfall
(C) Rainfall (D) Clouds

9. Socks is related to 'Nylon, in the same way as 'Purse' is related to __________.
   (A) Money (B) Leather
   (C) Locker (D) Coins
10. 'Doctor' is related to 'Patient' in the same way as 'Lawyer' is related to _________.
   (A) Customer (B) Criminal
   (C) Magistrate (D) Client

Direction: Three out of four options given below are alike in a certain way and form a group. Choose the one that does not belong to the group?

11. (A) Pen (B) Toy
   (C) Eraser (D) Sharpener
12. (A) Apple (B) Jack fruit
   (C) Banana (D) Water-melon
13. (A) Horse cart (B) Bus
   (C) Tractor (D) Truck
14. (A) Tree (B) Root
   (C) Trunk (D) Leaf
15. (A) Pigeon (B) Crow
   (C) Bird (D) Koel

Direction: Choose the correct option.

16. If in a certain code 'VIJAYA' is written as 'AYAJIV' then how SHARMA can be written in that code?
   (A) AMRHAS (B) ARMAHS
   (C) AMRAHS (D) RAMAHS
17. If in a certain code READ is written as 'TGCF' then how TEACH can be written in that code?
   (A) VGECJ (B) VGCEJ
   (C) UFBDI (D) VCGEJ
18. If EARTH is coded as SUBDZ, then how TEAR can be written in that code?
   (A) BSUD (B) DUSB
   (C) BSDU (D) DSUB
19. If BHASHA is written as 154754 and BRAIN is written as 13408, then AHINSA can be written as
   (A) 405847 (B) 450847
   (C) 458074 (D) 450874
20. If HKUJ is written as FISH in a code language, then how is UVCD written in that code?
   (A) STAB (B) STAR
   (C) STAF (D) STAK
21. Vijay started from school and walked 2 Km straight towards South. He then turned left and travelled 3 Km. He then again turned left and travelled 2 km straight. How far is he from his school?
   (A) 3 Km (B) 4 Km
   (C) 5 Km (D) 6 Km
22. Huma walks 6 Km South and then turns left and walks 4 Km straight. He again turns left and walks 5 Km. In which direction is his face now?
   (A) East (B) West
   (C) North (D) South
23. Four people Vijay, Munesh, Kailash and Moolchand are playing cards. Kailash and Moolchond are in same pair. Vijay's face is towards North. If Kailash's face is towards West, then whose face will be towards south?
   (A) Moolchand (B) Munesh
   (C) Kailash (D) None of these
24. Rashmi walks 2 Km towards west, then she walks 10 Km towards North and then again 4 Km towards West and she finally walks 18 Km towards South. How far is she from her starting point.
   (A) 10 Km (B) 18 Km
   (C) 16 Km (D) 12 Km
25. If North-East becomes South then what will be the direction of South-West?
   (A) East (B) West
   (C) North (D) South

Direction (26–30): Choose the correct option.

26. In a class of 20 students, Jai has fifth position from top. What is his position from bottom?
   (A) 14 (B) 15
   (C) 16 (D) 17

27. Some students are standing in a row. Shiv Kumar was standing at twentieth position from right and tenth position from left. What is the number of students in that row?

(A) 29 (B) 30
(C) 31 (D) 28

28. Rashmi, Sandeep, Khyati and Vijay are sitting on a bench. Next to Khyati towards left Vijay is sitting. On one side of Sandeep is Khyati and on other side is Mannu. Who is sitting at extreme right?

(A) Rashmi
(B) Sandeep
(C) Khyati
(D) Vijay

29. Jaideep is the 20th from either end of a row of boys. How many boys are there in that row?

(A) 40 (B) 39
(C) 38 (D) 41

30. There is a group of five villages. Khan pura is smaller than Bhiroli. Jadaul is bigger than Bamanpur and Jugsana is bigger than Bhiroli but not as big as Bamanpur. Which is the biggest village?

(A) Khanpura
(B) Bhiroli
(C) Jadaul
(D) Bamanpur

Directions (31–33): Choose the correct option.

31. How many pairs of letters in the word 'DEBUT' have as many letters between them in the word as in the alphabet?

(A) No
(B) One
(C) Two
(D) Three

32. How many pairs of letters in the word 'DONATION' have as many letters between them as there are in the alphabet?

(A) One (B) Two
(C) Three (D) Four

33. If it is possible to make a word with 2nd, 5th, 9th and 11th letters in the word 'SUPERFLUOUS'. Write the first letter of that word.

(A) P
(B) S
(C) R
(D) None of these

Directions (34–35): Arrange the given words in the sequence in which they occur in the dictionary and then choose the correct sequence.

34. 1. Selection 2. Seldom
3. Sender 4. Self
5. Sell

(A) 42315 (B) 13524
(C) 21453 (D) 24153

35. 1. Long 2. Lost
3. Load 4. Longing
5. Loose

(A) 31452 (B) 14325
(C) 34152 (D) 31425

Directions (36–37): Read the following passage and answer the given questions.

P,Q,R and S are sitting around a table. P sits opposite to teacher. Q sits right of artist. S sits opposite to R. Doctor sits on the left of engineer.

36. What is the profession of P?

(A) Teacher
(B) Engineer
(C) Doctor
(D) Artist

37. What is the profession of Q?

(A) Artist
(B) Doctor
(C) Engineer
(D) Teacher

Directions (38–40): Read the following information carefully and answer the questions that follow.

Five friends Sulekha, Kanchan, Madhu,

Anju and Radha were standing for a photo in front of camera. Sulekha is taller than Radha. Anju is a little shorter than Kanchan but little taller than Sulekha. Radha is shorter than Sulekha. Madhu is the tallest among all.

38. Who is the second tallest?
    (A) Kanchan
    (B) Anju
    (C) Radha
    (D) Sulekha
39. Who is taller than Anju but shorter than Madhu?
    (A) Anju
    (B) Radha
    (C) Sulekha
    (D) Kanchan
40. Who is the shortest among all girls?
    (A) Sulekha
    (B) Kanchan
    (C) Radha
    (D) Anju

Directions (41–45): Select the correct option which exactly matches with the mirror image of the letter/word/number figure given in the question.

41. R
    (A) Я (B) ꓤ
    (C) R (D) ꓤ
42. KHYATI
    (A) IꓕAYHK (B) ITAYHK
    (C) ITAYHK (D) ITAYHK
43.

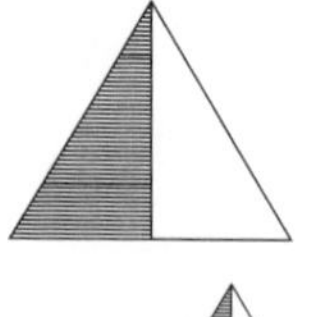

(A) 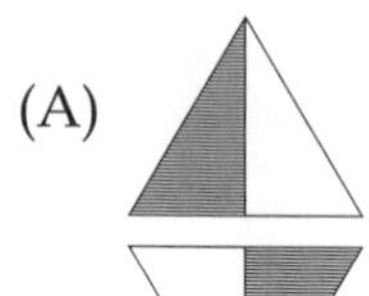 (B) 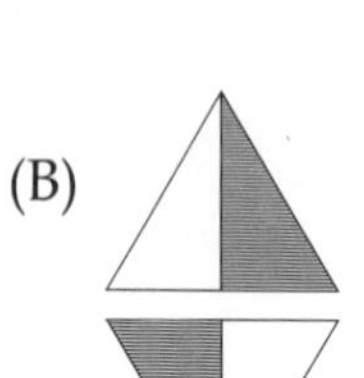

(C) (D) 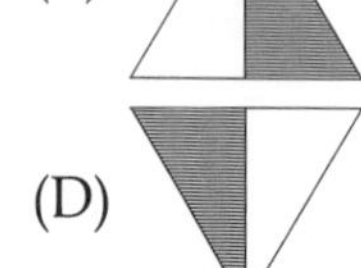

44.

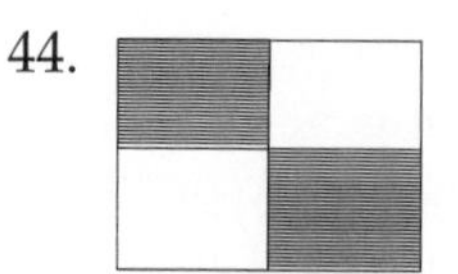

(A) 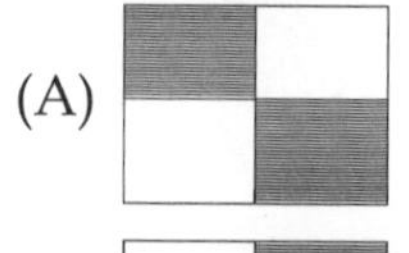 (B) 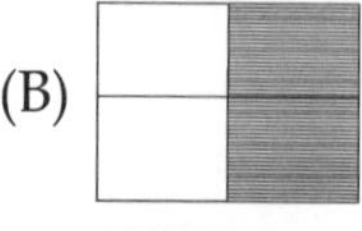

(C)  (D) 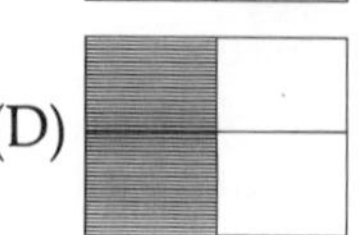

45.

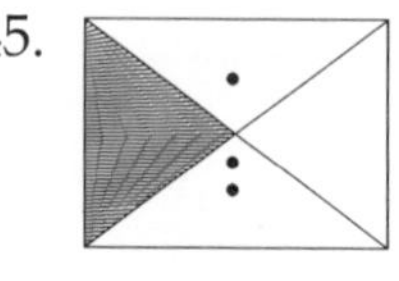

(A) 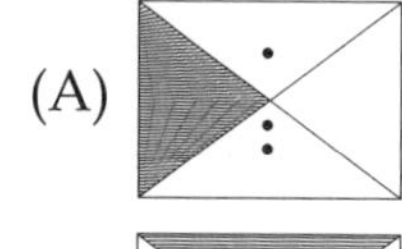 (B) 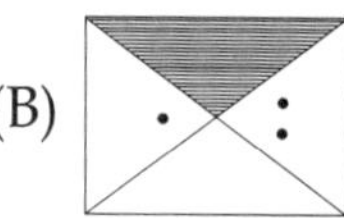

(C) 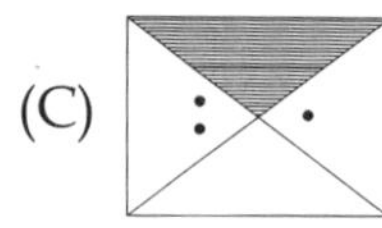 (D) 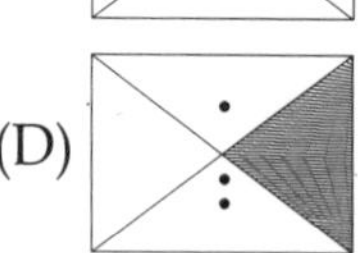

Directions (46–50): Choose the alternative which shows the correct water image of the given word.

46. V I J A Y
    (A) YAᒐIV (B) VIᒐAY
    (C) ΛIᒋ∀⅄ (D) ⅄∀ᒋIΛ
47. SHARMA
    (A) SHARMA (B) AMRAHS
    (C) SHARMA (D) AMЯAHS
48. DELHI
    (A) DEΓHI (B) DƎΓHI
    (C) DƎᒧHI (D) DƎLHI
49. MEERUT
    (A) TURƎƎM (B) MEERUꓕ
    (C) TUЯƎƎM (D) MƎƎRUꓕ
50. BULANDSHAHR
    (A) BUᒧ ANDSHAHR
    (B) BUΓANDSHAHЯ
    (C) BUΓANDSHAHR
    (D) BUΓAND SHAHR

Directions (51–55): The fig (X) is embedded in any one of the four alternatives figures (A), (B), (C) and (D). Find the alternative which contains figure (D) as its part.

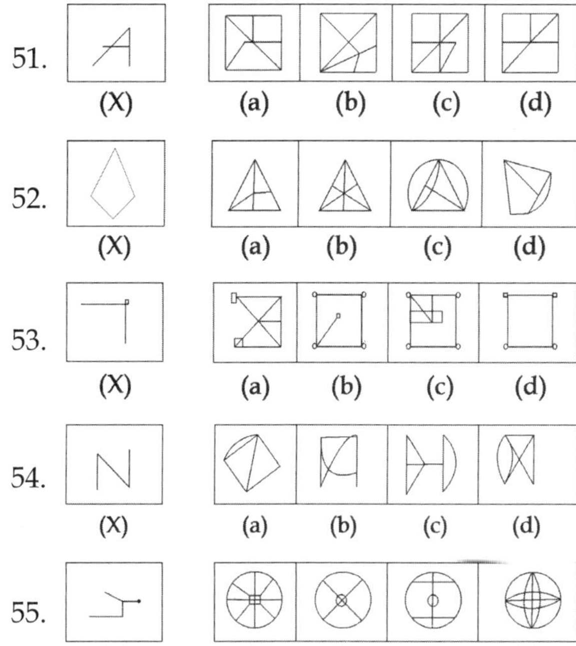

56. How many squares does the following figure have?

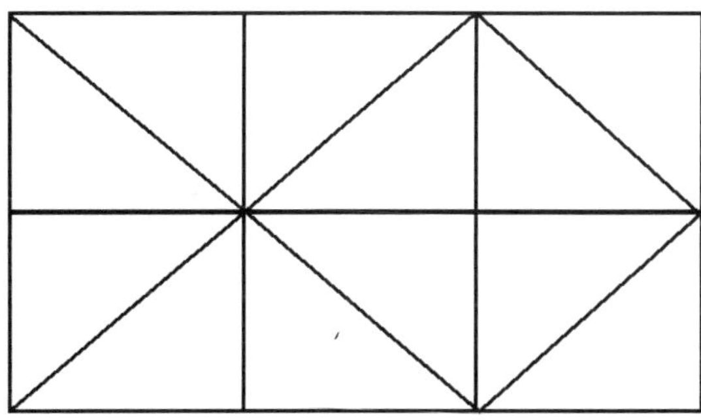

(A) 7
(B) 9
(C) 8
(D) 10

57. How many parallelograms does the following figure have?

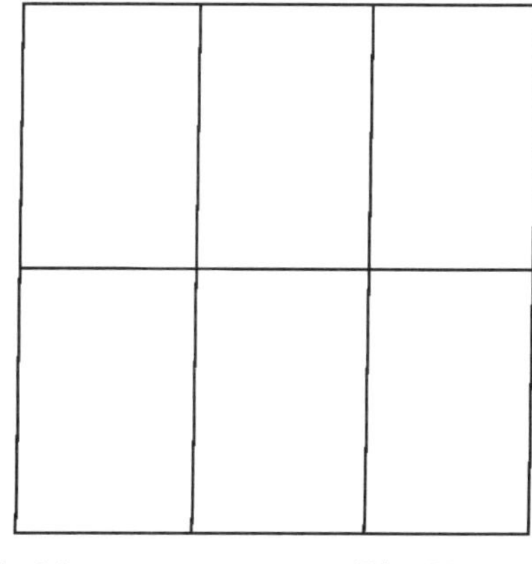

(A) 14 (B) 17
(C) 18 (D) 16

58. How many triangles does the following figure have?

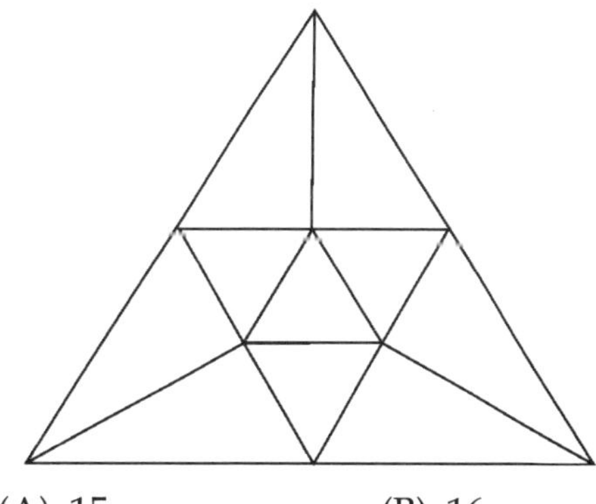

(A) 15 (B) 16
(C) 17 (D) 12

59. How many triangles and squares does the following figure have?

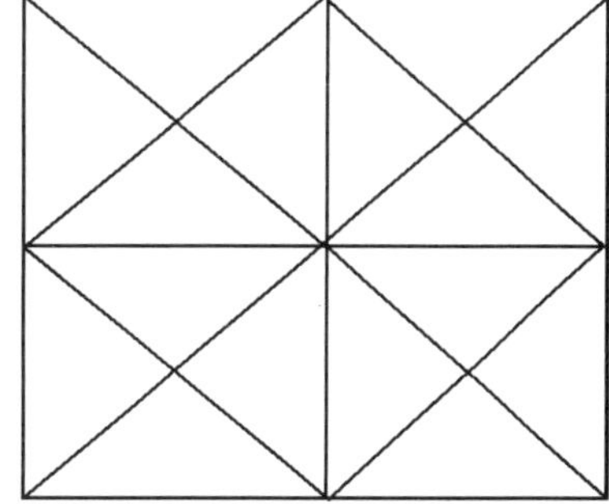

(A) 44 Triangles, 10 Squares
(B) 42 Triangles, 12 Squares
(C) 40 Triangles, 7 Squares
(D) 24 Triangles, 14 Squares

60. How many straight lines does the following figure have?

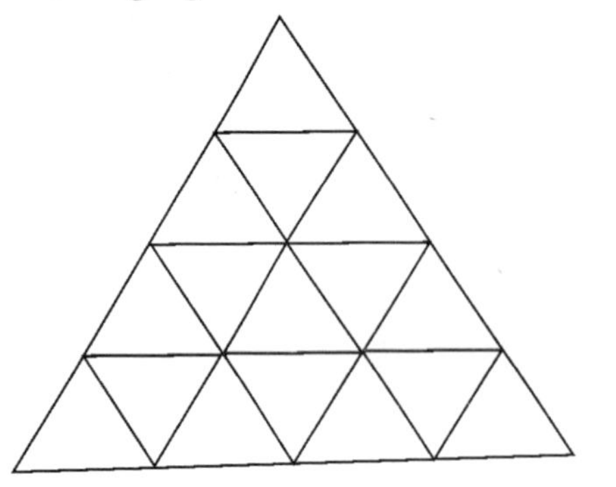

(A) 10
(B) 11
(C) 12
(D) 14

Darken Your Choice with HB Pencil

1.	Ⓐ	Ⓑ	Ⓒ	Ⓓ	13.	Ⓐ	Ⓑ	Ⓒ	Ⓓ	25.	Ⓐ	Ⓑ	Ⓒ	Ⓓ	37	Ⓐ	Ⓑ	Ⓒ	Ⓓ	49.	Ⓐ	Ⓑ	Ⓒ	Ⓓ
2.	Ⓐ	Ⓑ	Ⓒ	Ⓓ	14.	Ⓐ	Ⓑ	Ⓒ	Ⓓ	26.	Ⓐ	Ⓑ	Ⓒ	Ⓓ	38.	Ⓐ	Ⓑ	Ⓒ	Ⓓ	50.	Ⓐ	Ⓑ	Ⓒ	Ⓓ
3.	Ⓐ	Ⓑ	Ⓒ	Ⓓ	15.	Ⓐ	Ⓑ	Ⓒ	Ⓓ	27.	Ⓐ	Ⓑ	Ⓒ	Ⓓ	39.	Ⓐ	Ⓑ	Ⓒ	Ⓓ	51.	Ⓐ	Ⓑ	Ⓒ	Ⓓ
4.	Ⓐ	Ⓑ	Ⓒ	Ⓓ	16.	Ⓐ	Ⓑ	Ⓒ	Ⓓ	28.	Ⓐ	Ⓑ	Ⓒ	Ⓓ	40.	Ⓐ	Ⓑ	Ⓒ	Ⓓ	52.	Ⓐ	Ⓑ	Ⓒ	Ⓓ
5.	Ⓐ	Ⓑ	Ⓒ	Ⓓ	17.	Ⓐ	Ⓑ	Ⓒ	Ⓓ	29.	Ⓐ	Ⓑ	Ⓒ	Ⓓ	41.	Ⓐ	Ⓑ	Ⓒ	Ⓓ	53.	Ⓐ	Ⓑ	Ⓒ	Ⓓ
6.	Ⓐ	Ⓑ	Ⓒ	Ⓓ	18.	Ⓐ	Ⓑ	Ⓒ	Ⓓ	30.	Ⓐ	Ⓑ	Ⓒ	Ⓓ	42.	Ⓐ	Ⓑ	Ⓒ	Ⓓ	54.	Ⓐ	Ⓑ	Ⓒ	Ⓓ
7.	Ⓐ	Ⓑ	Ⓒ	Ⓓ	19.	Ⓐ	Ⓑ	Ⓒ	Ⓓ	31.	Ⓐ	Ⓑ	Ⓒ	Ⓓ	43.	Ⓐ	Ⓑ	Ⓒ	Ⓓ	55.	Ⓐ	Ⓑ	Ⓒ	Ⓓ
8.	Ⓐ	Ⓑ	Ⓒ	Ⓓ	20.	Ⓐ	Ⓑ	Ⓒ	Ⓓ	32.	Ⓐ	Ⓑ	Ⓒ	Ⓓ	44.	Ⓐ	Ⓑ	Ⓒ	Ⓓ	56.	Ⓐ	Ⓑ	Ⓒ	Ⓓ
9.	Ⓐ	Ⓑ	Ⓒ	Ⓓ	21.	Ⓐ	Ⓑ	Ⓒ	Ⓓ	33.	Ⓐ	Ⓑ	Ⓒ	Ⓓ	45.	Ⓐ	Ⓑ	Ⓒ	Ⓓ	57.	Ⓐ	Ⓑ	Ⓒ	Ⓓ
10.	Ⓐ	Ⓑ	Ⓒ	Ⓓ	22.	Ⓐ	Ⓑ	Ⓒ	Ⓓ	34.	Ⓐ	Ⓑ	Ⓒ	Ⓓ	46.	Ⓐ	Ⓑ	Ⓒ	Ⓓ	58.	Ⓐ	Ⓑ	Ⓒ	Ⓓ
11.	Ⓐ	Ⓑ	Ⓒ	Ⓓ	23.	Ⓐ	Ⓑ	Ⓒ	Ⓓ	35.	Ⓐ	Ⓑ	Ⓒ	Ⓓ	47.	Ⓐ	Ⓑ	Ⓒ	Ⓓ	59.	Ⓐ	Ⓑ	Ⓒ	Ⓓ
12.	Ⓐ	Ⓑ	Ⓒ	Ⓓ	24.	Ⓐ	Ⓑ	Ⓒ	Ⓓ	36.	Ⓐ	Ⓑ	Ⓒ	Ⓓ	48.	Ⓐ	Ⓑ	Ⓒ	Ⓓ	60.	Ⓐ	Ⓑ	Ⓒ	Ⓓ

MODEL TEST PAPER

MULTIPLE CHOICE QUESTIONS

1. Choose the correct option to complete the given series.
   3 8 13 18 23 28 33 ? ?
   (A) 39 44 (B) 38 44
   (C) 38 43 (D) 37 42

2. Choose the correct option to complete the given series.
   20 20 17 17 14 14 11 ? ?
   (A) 8 8 (B) 11 8
   (C) 11 14 (D) 8 9

3. Choose the correct option to complete the given series.
   BCB, DED, FGF, HIH, ___
   (A) JKJ (B) HJH
   (C) IJI (D) JHJ

4. Choose the odd one out from the given options.
   (A) December (B) February
   (C) March (D) July

5. Choose the odd one out from the given options.
   (A) Grapes (B) Pineapple
   (C) Cashew (D) Apple

6. Choose the odd one out from the given options.
   (A) Tomato (B) Cucumber
   (C) Peas (D) Potato

7. Find the answer figure which comes next in the series given in the problem figures.

Problem figure

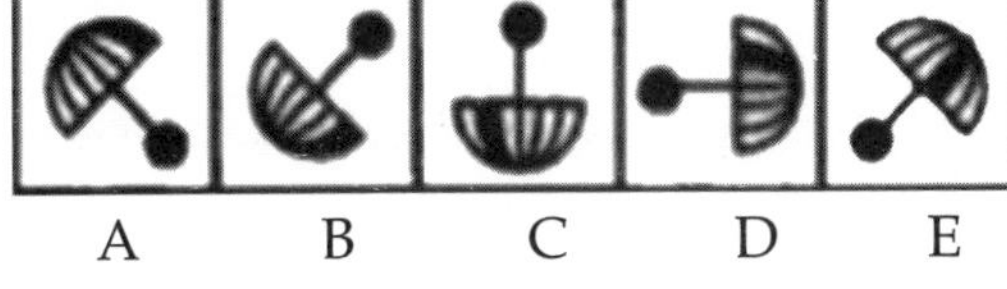

A B C D E

Answer figure

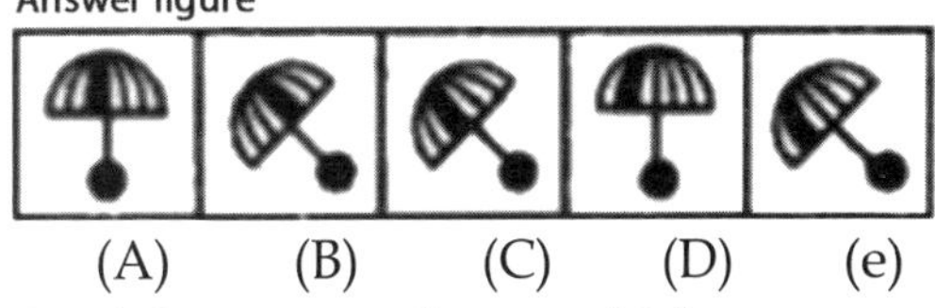

(A) (B) (C) (D) (e)

8. Find the answer figure which comes next in the series given in the problem figures.

Problem figure

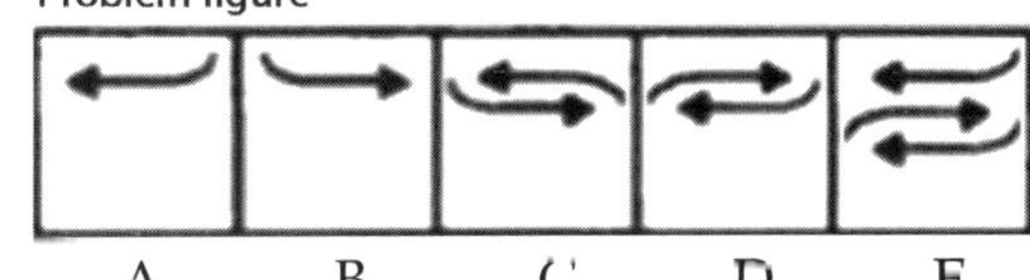

A B C D E

Answer figure

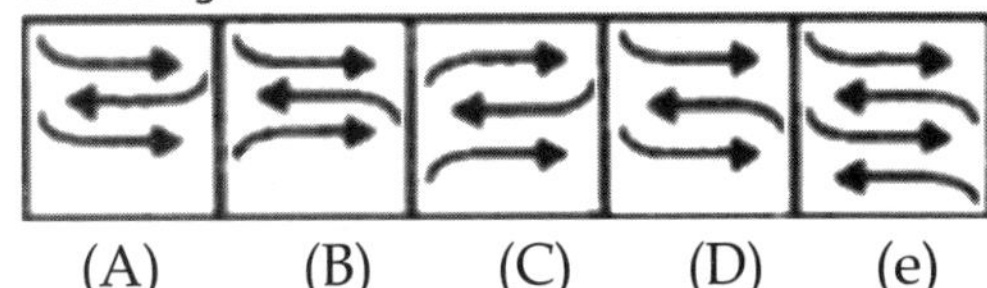

(A) (B) (C) (D) (e)

9. Choose the alternative which most closely resembles the mirror image of the given figure (X).

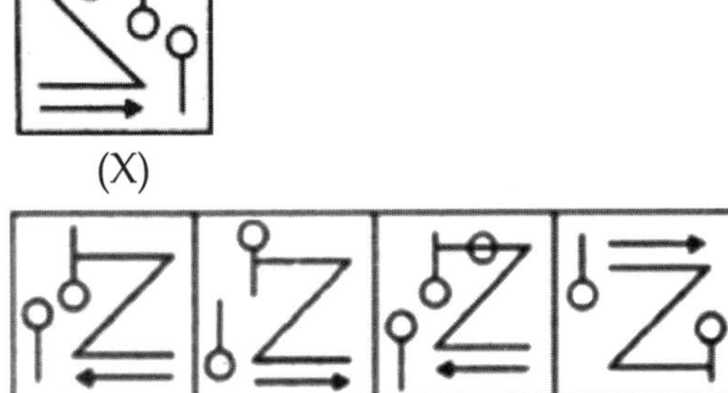

(X)

(A) (B) (C) (D)

10. Choose the alternative which most closely resembles the mirror image of the given figure (X).

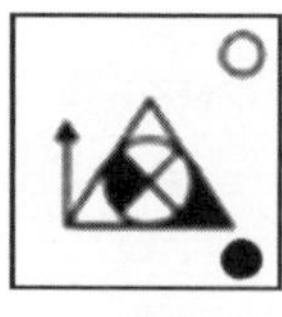

(X)

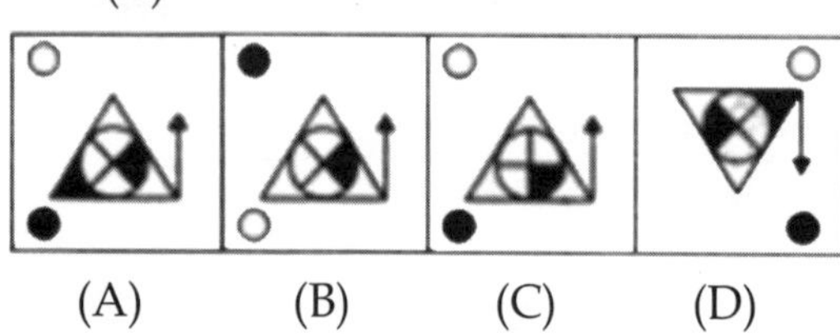

(A) (B) (C) (D)

11. Which is the correct statement about the instinctive behaviour of animals?
    (A) It is a complex pattern of innate behaviour.
    (B) It begins when the animal recognizes a stimulus.
    (C) It takes hardly a few hours to complete.
    (D) Both (A) and (B)

12. Which two of the following animals are both primary consumers?

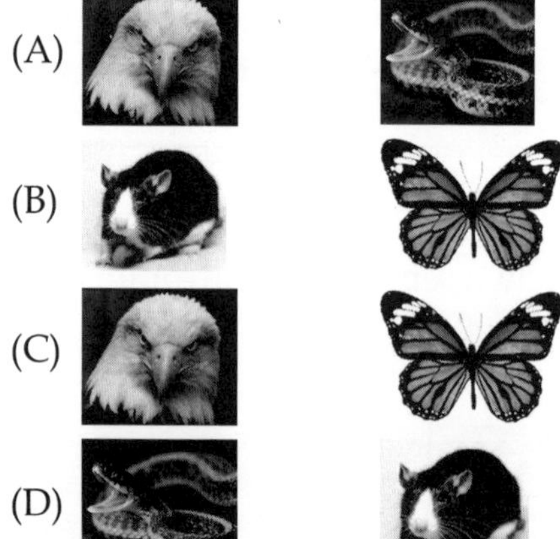

13. We all know that green plants have chlorophyll and without chlorophyll, photosynthesis cannot take place.
    How do croton plants, which are red in colour, prepare their food?
    (A) Croton plants have chlorophyll, but they appear dark red because it is hidden by the dark red colour.
    (B) Croton plants are dark red in colour and do not contain chlorophyll.
    (C) Croton plants do not contain chlorophyll so they appear red.
    (D) Croton plants do not contain chlorophyll but can still make their own food.

14. Which of the following instruments is used to examine the cells of a leaf?
    (A) Microscope
    (B) Camera
    (C) Magnifying glass
    (D) Telescope

15. Teacher asked the class, 'In which parts of the digestive system can digestive juices be found?' Some of her pupils gave the following answers. Which of the answers is correct?
    (A) Sanchit: gullet and large intestine
    (B) Ananya: mouth, gullet, and stomach
    (C) Rachit: mouth, stomach, and small intestine
    (D) Shreya: stomach, small intestine, and large intestine

16. From smallest to largest, which two of these are in the wrong order?
    (i) Organelle: Parts inside the cell that help the cell function.
    (ii) Organism: A single being in a population.
    (iii) Organ system: All the systems in the organism.
    (iv) Tissue: Parts of an organ with specific jobs.
    (v) Organ: Parts of the organ system that work together.
    (A) None
    (B) (i) and (iv)
    (C) (ii) and (iii)
    (D) (v) and (iii)

17. Which part(s) of the human eye is/are incorrectly labelled?

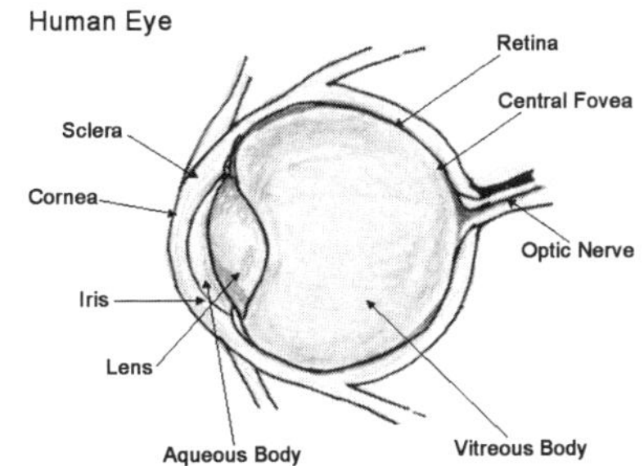

(A) Pupil, cornea, and retina
(B) Pupil only
(C) Lens, retina, cornea, and pupil
(D) Pupils and lens only

18. Some candidates are practicing running for the Independence Day competition. If they want to gain energy quickly then which of the following should they take?
(A) Minerals (B) Vitamins
(C) Carbohydrates (D) Fats

19. Nutrients which are called protective foods are ______.
(A) Vitamins and minerals
(B) Carbohydrates
(C) Proteins
(D) Fats and carbohydrates

20. The tiny pores present on the leaves of the plants are called ______.
(A) Chlorophyll (B) Cells
(C) Stomata (D) Grains

21. Rain and snow are the two forms of ______.
(A) Water (B) Fresh water
(C) Salt water (D) Precipitation

22. A place's ______ is the pattern of weather over many years.
(A) Temperature (B) Humidity
(C) Heat (D) Climate

23. The protection of natural resources, including water, is called ______.
(A) Humus (B) Organic
(C) Inorganic (D) Conservation

24. The process of changing from a liquid state to a gaseous state is called ______.
(A) Sublimation (B) Condensation
(C) Evaporation (D) Precipitation

25. A magnet is ______.
(A) A wooden figure
(B) An object that attracts, or pulls on certain materials like iron and steel
(C) A magnetic force
(D) A metal figure

26. Four pupils made the following remarks about magnets. Which of these pupils has made the correct remark about magnets?
Rachit: Magnets are only made of iron.
Ananya: Every magnet has only two poles.
Shreya: Objects made of nickel can be attracted to a magnet.
Sanchit: Magnets always come to rest in a North-East direction.
(A) Sanchit and Rachit
(B) Ananya and Shreya
(C) Shreya and Rachit
(D) John and Bala

27. From the smallest to the largest, which is the correct order of size?
(A) Sun, earth, milky way galaxy
(B) Earth, sun, milky way galaxy
(C) Earth, milky way galaxy, sun
(D) Milky way galaxy, sun, earth

28. Observe the diagram and indicate the four cardinal directions.
Now, fill in the blanks with the phrases: on the right hand side of, on the left hand side of, in front of, behind.

North is ______ the girl.
South is ______ the girl.
East is on the ______ the girl.
West is ______ the girl.
(A) Behind; in front of; on the left hand side of; on the right hand side of
(B) On the left hand side of; on the right hand side of; behind; in front of

(C) In front of; behind; on the left hand side of; on the right hand side of
(D) On the right hand side of; on the right hand side of; in front of; behind

29. A see-saw is an example of which simple machine?
(A) Wedge (B) Lever
(C) Inclined plane (D) Screw

30. The bubbles that come out rapidly when we open a soda water bottle are ________.
(A) Carbon dioxide bubbles
(B) Nitrogen bubbles
(C) Water bubbles
(D) Oxygen bubbles

31. The inter-molecular space is more in ________.
(A) Iron (B) Water
(C) Mercury (D) Hydrogen

32. Radio converts ________.
(A) Mechanical energy into electrical energy
(B) Electrical energy into kinetic energy
(C) Electrical energy into sound energy
(D) Geothermal energy into heat energy

33. Municipal solid waste is often called ________.
(A) Biodegradable waste
(B) Garbage
(C) Non-biodegradable waste
(D) Domestic waste

34. What is the minimum required hemoglobin in the human body?
(A) 11 gm/dl (B) 12 gm/dl
(C) 16 gm/dl (D) 8.5 gm/dl

35. Complete the following table with the correct information.

Measurement	International Unit	Symbol
Length		
Time		
Temperature		

(A) Liter, L; second, s; kelvin, °K
(B) Meter, m; second s; kelvin, °K
(C) Second, s; kelvin, °K; liter, L
(D) Liter, L; second, s; kelvin, °C

36. A dark-coloured substance formed from dead remains of plants and animals is called ________.
(A) Clay (B) Humus
(C) Gravel (D) Loam

37. Which of the following are non-conventional sources of energy?
(A) Coal and solar radiators
(B) Solar radiators and nuclear plant's generated electricity
(C) Petroleum and coal
(D) Petroleum and nuclear plant's generated electricity

38. If there is no rain, crops will fail to grow. This condition will lead to ________.
(A) Famine
(B) Flood
(C) Drought
(D) Both (A) and (B)

39. Which of these materials is a good insulating material for ice-cubes because it does not conduct heat well?
(A) Silver (B) Iron
(C) Plastic (D) Gold

40. Which group makes up nearly all the energy presently used in the county?

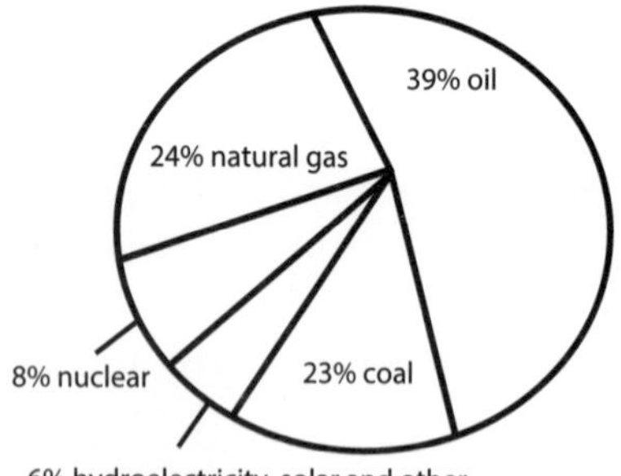

(A) Fissile fuel
(B) Coal and nuclear
(C) Oil and gas
(D) Nuclear, hydroelectricity, solar as other sources

41. Geeta's teacher gave her four samples and asked her to categorise them under different mixture categories.

Geeta's observations:

Sample P: It was a liquid sample with some particles settled at the bottom.

Sample Q: It was a liquid sample with a layer of one yellow-coloured liquid at the top.

Sample R: It was a white liquid with no settled particles.

Sample S: It was liquid sample with a pink layer at the top.

What type of mixtures are the samples?

(A) P: Homogenous solid in liquid mixture; Q: Emulsion; R: Homogenous mixture; S: Heterogeneous mixture

(B) P: Heterogeneous solid in liquid mixture; Q: Emulsion; R: Homogenous mixture; S: Heterogeneous mixture

(C) P: Homogenous solid in liquid mixture; Q: Emulsion; R: Heterogeneous mixture; S: Emulsion

(D) P: Heterogeneous solid in liquid mixture; Q: Emulsion; R: Homogenous mixture; S: Emulsion

42. What could be the best suited explanation for the statement: "Survival of the fittest" in terms of animal adaptation?

(A) The strongest animal is the fittest to survive

(B) Carnivores are the fittest to survive

(C) Plants and animals with the traits best suited to their environment are the fittest to survive

(D) Only plants are the fittest to survive

43. A group of children held a discussion related to plant pollination and the role of flowers. Read their observations and categorise how many children were correct and how many were not.

Child	Perception (Regarding Plant Pollination and Flowers)
P	The flower attracts pollinator through its nectar.
Q	Bees and hummingbirds are the only pollinators.
R	Bright colours of flowers attract pollinators.
S	Flowers open in night to attract nocturnal pollinators.

(A) Only P is correct

(B) Only S is correct

(C) Only Q is wrong

(D) Only R is correct

44. What could be the possible reason for the query raised: How does the moon reflect the sun's light but the things on the earth (like rocks) do not reflect the sun's light?

(A) The moon has shiny surface, this is the reason it reflects the sunlight.

(B) The moon is big so it reflects the sunlight.

(C) The moon rotates around the earth this is the reason why it reflects the sunlight.

(D) The statement is incorrect; everything reflects sunlight and if something does not reflect light, it looks completely black.

45. Children of class 5 attempted to enlist the steps of the lifecycle of a rock. They all made it incomplete. Join the fragments made by them to make the complete lifecycle of a rock.

Child	Rock's Lifecycle Stages
L	Burial and Compaction, Deformation
M	Metamorphism, Uplift
N	Weathering, Erosion and Transport, Deposition
O	Melting and Crystallisation of Magma

Which is the correct sequence?

(A) N, M, O, L (B) L, M, N, O

(C) N, L, M, O (D) N, L, O, M

46. It takes about ________ days for the Moon to complete its cycle of phases.
    (A) 27.5 (B) 28.5
    (C) 29.5 (D) 30.5
47. Which of the following is true for the molecules of gases?
    (A) They can move around freely
    (B) They have a fixed volume
    (C) They have a fixed shape
    (D) They cannot move freely
48. Drainage water is also used for irrigation. It is a ________.
    (A) Surface water source
    (B) Non-conventional source
    (C) Dirty water
    (D) Ground water
49. A simple machine ________.
    (A) Is used to make work easier
    (B) Has an engine
    (C) Is simple because it is easy to use
    (D) Is not actually simple to use
50. Which of the following set represents primary consumers?
    (A) Cows and giraffes
    (B) Buffaloes and cats
    (C) Insects and butterflies
    (D) All of these

Darken Your Choice with HB Pencil

1.	Ⓐ	Ⓑ	Ⓒ	Ⓓ	11.	Ⓐ	Ⓑ	Ⓒ	Ⓓ	21.	Ⓐ	Ⓑ	Ⓒ	Ⓓ	31	Ⓐ	Ⓑ	Ⓒ	Ⓓ	41.	Ⓐ	Ⓑ	Ⓒ	Ⓓ
2.	Ⓐ	Ⓑ	Ⓒ	Ⓓ	12.	Ⓐ	Ⓑ	Ⓒ	Ⓓ	22.	Ⓐ	Ⓑ	Ⓒ	Ⓓ	32.	Ⓐ	Ⓑ	Ⓒ	Ⓓ	42.	Ⓐ	Ⓑ	Ⓒ	Ⓓ
3.	Ⓐ	Ⓑ	Ⓒ	Ⓓ	13.	Ⓐ	Ⓑ	Ⓒ	Ⓓ	23.	Ⓐ	Ⓑ	Ⓒ	Ⓓ	33.	Ⓐ	Ⓑ	Ⓒ	Ⓓ	43.	Ⓐ	Ⓑ	Ⓒ	Ⓓ
4.	Ⓐ	Ⓑ	Ⓒ	Ⓓ	14.	Ⓐ	Ⓑ	Ⓒ	Ⓓ	24.	Ⓐ	Ⓑ	Ⓒ	Ⓓ	34.	Ⓐ	Ⓑ	Ⓒ	Ⓓ	44.	Ⓐ	Ⓑ	Ⓒ	Ⓓ
5.	Ⓐ	Ⓑ	Ⓒ	Ⓓ	15.	Ⓐ	Ⓑ	Ⓒ	Ⓓ	25.	Ⓐ	Ⓑ	Ⓒ	Ⓓ	35.	Ⓐ	Ⓑ	Ⓒ	Ⓓ	45.	Ⓐ	Ⓑ	Ⓒ	Ⓓ
6.	Ⓐ	Ⓑ	Ⓒ	Ⓓ	16.	Ⓐ	Ⓑ	Ⓒ	Ⓓ	26.	Ⓐ	Ⓑ	Ⓒ	Ⓓ	36.	Ⓐ	Ⓑ	Ⓒ	Ⓓ	46.	Ⓐ	Ⓑ	Ⓒ	Ⓓ
7.	Ⓐ	Ⓑ	Ⓒ	Ⓓ	17.	Ⓐ	Ⓑ	Ⓒ	Ⓓ	27.	Ⓐ	Ⓑ	Ⓒ	Ⓓ	37.	Ⓐ	Ⓑ	Ⓒ	Ⓓ	47.	Ⓐ	Ⓑ	Ⓒ	Ⓓ
8.	Ⓐ	Ⓑ	Ⓒ	Ⓓ	18.	Ⓐ	Ⓑ	Ⓒ	Ⓓ	28.	Ⓐ	Ⓑ	Ⓒ	Ⓓ	38.	Ⓐ	Ⓑ	Ⓒ	Ⓓ	48.	Ⓐ	Ⓑ	Ⓒ	Ⓓ
9.	Ⓐ	Ⓑ	Ⓒ	Ⓓ	19.	Ⓐ	Ⓑ	Ⓒ	Ⓓ	29.	Ⓐ	Ⓑ	Ⓒ	Ⓓ	39.	Ⓐ	Ⓑ	Ⓒ	Ⓓ	49.	Ⓐ	Ⓑ	Ⓒ	Ⓓ
10.	Ⓐ	Ⓑ	Ⓒ	Ⓓ	20.	Ⓐ	Ⓑ	Ⓒ	Ⓓ	30.	Ⓐ	Ⓑ	Ⓒ	Ⓓ	40.	Ⓐ	Ⓑ	Ⓒ	Ⓓ	50.	Ⓐ	Ⓑ	Ⓒ	Ⓓ

HINTS AND SOLUTIONS

1. ANIMALS

Answer Key

1. (D)	2. (C)	3. (D)	4. (D)	5. (A)	6. (D)	7. (C)	8. (D)	9. (D)	10. (C)
11. (B)	12. (D)	13. (A)	14. (D)	15. (C)	16. (D)	17. (C)	18. (B)	19. (D)	20. (C)
21. (C)	22. (B)	23. (B)	24. (B)	25. (B)					

HOTS (ACHIEVERS SECTION)

1. (B)	2. (B)	3. (B)	4. (C)	5. (C)

2. HUMAN BODY AND HEALTH

Answer Key

1. (D)	2. (C)	3. (C)	4. (D)	5. (B)	6. (A)	7. (D)	8. (D)	9. (D)	10. (C)
11. (C)	12. (B)	13. (A)	14. (A)	15. (D)	16. (A)	17. (B)	18. (C)	19. (B)	20. (A)
21. (D)	22. (C)	23. (D)	24. (B)	25. (D)	26. (B)	27. (C)	28. (B)	29. (D)	30. (B)

HOTS (ACHIEVERS SECTION)

31. (B)	32. (D)	33. (D)	34. (D)	35. (A)	36. (C)	37. (B)	38. (C)	39. (A)	40. (A)

3. PLANT LIFE

Answer Key

1. (A)	2. (B)	3. (D)	4. (C)	5. (B)	6. (D)	7. (A)	8. (D)	9. (B)	10. (D)
11. (C)	12. (B)	13. (B)	14. (A)	15. (A)	16. (D)	17. (D)	18. (B)	19. (B)	20. (B)
21. (B)	22. (B)	23. (B)	24. (C)	25. (C)					

HOTS (ACHIEVERS SECTION)

26. (B)	27. (D)	28. (D)	29. (D)	30. (C)

4. NATURAL RESOURCES AND CALAMITIES

Answer Key

1. (B)	2. (B)	3. (C)	4. (D)	5. (B)	6. (B)	7. (C)	8. (C)	9. (D)	10. (B)
11. (D)	12. (B)	13. (A)	14. (B)	15. (D)	16. (A)	17. (D)	18. (A)	19. (A)	20. (D)
21. (D)	22. (A)	23. (A)	24. (A)	25. (A)	26. (C)	27. (C)	28. (B)	29. (A)	30. (D)

HOTS (ACHIEVERS SECTION)

31. (C)	32. (C)	33. (C)	34. (B)	35. (B)

5. WATER

Answer Key

1. (D)	2. (B)	3. (B)	4. (A)	5. (D)	6. (B)	7. (C)	8. (B)	9. (A)	10. (C)
11. (B)	12. (B)	13. (B)	14. (D)	15. (C)	16. (A)	17. (A)	18. (B)	19. (B)	20. (B)
21. (C)	22. (C)	23. (B)	24. (A)	25. (D)					

HOTS (ACHIEVERS SECTION)

26. (A)	27. (D)	28. (D)	29. (B)	30. (D)

6. EARTH AND UNIVERSE

Answer Key

1. (C)	2. (A)	3. (B)	4. (C)	5. (C)	6. (C)	7. (B)	8. (A)	9. (B)	10. (D)
11. (B)	12. (C)	13. (B)	14. (D)	15. (D)	16. (C)	17. (A)	18. (D)	19. (A)	20. (B)
21. (B)	22. (B)	23. (C)	24. (C)	25. (C)					

HOTS (ACHIEVERS SECTION)

26. (A)	27. (B)	28. (C)	29. (C)	30. (D)

7. MATTER AND MATERIALS

Answer Key

1. (A)	2. (B)	3. (A)	4. (B)	5. (B)	6. (B)	7. (A)	8. (B)	9. (B)	10. (B)
11. (C)	12. (D)	13. (A)	14. (A)	15. (C)	16. (B)	17. (C)	18. (C)	19. (D)	20. (B)
21. (A)	22. (C)	23. (B)	24. (D)	25. (B)	26. (B)	27. (A)	28. (B)	29. (B)	30. (D)

HOTS (ACHIEVERS SECTION)

31. (A)	32. (C)	33. (D)	34. (A)	35. (C)

8. FORCE, WORK AND ENERGY

Answer Key

1. (B)	2. (C)	3. (A)	4. (A)	5. (D)	6. (D)	7. (C)	8. (A)	9. (A)	10. (C)
11. (B)	12. (B)	13. (B)	14. (C)	15. (B)	16. (A)	17. (A)	18. (A)	19. (D)	20. (B)
21. (D)	22. (C)	23. (A)	24. (A)	25. (C)	26. (D)	27. (C)	28. (A)	29. (D)	30. (D)

HOTS (ACHIEVERS SECTION)

1. (C)	2. (A)	3. (A)	4. (B)	5. (A)

9. ECOSYSTEM AND GENERAL SCIENCE

Answer Key

1. (A)	2. (D)	3. (A)	4. (C)	5. (C)	6. (B)	7. (C)	8. (B)	9. (C)	10. (A)
11. (D)	12. (D)	13. (A)	14. (D)	15. (D)	16. (D)	17. (C)	18. (C)	19. (B)	20. (C)
21. (A)	22. (B)	23. (A)	24. (D)	25. (D)	26. (D)	27. (C)	28. (D)	29. (C)	30. (B)

HOTS (ACHIEVERS SECTION)

31. (C)	32. (C)	33. (D)	34. (A)	35. (B)

10. LOGICAL REASONING

Answer Key

1. (C)	2. (B)	3. (A)	4. (D)	5. (A)	6. (A)	7. (B)	8. (C)	9. (B)	10. (D)
11. (B)	12. (B)	13. (A)	14. (A)	15. (C)	16. (C)	17. (B)	18. (D)	19. (D)	20. (A)
21. (A)	22. (C)	23. (B)	24. (A)	25. (C)	26. (C)	27. (A)	28. (A)	29. (B)	30. (C)
31. (D)	32. (C)	33. (B)	34. (C)	35. (A)	36. (B)	37. (D)	38. (A)	39. (D)	40. (C)
41. (A)	42. (D)	43. (B)	44. (C)	45. (D)	46. (C)	47. (C)	48. (A)	49. (B)	50. (C)
51. (D)	52. (B)	53. (D)	54. (A)	55. (A)	56. (B)	57. (C)	58. (A)	59. (A)	60. (C)

1. (C)

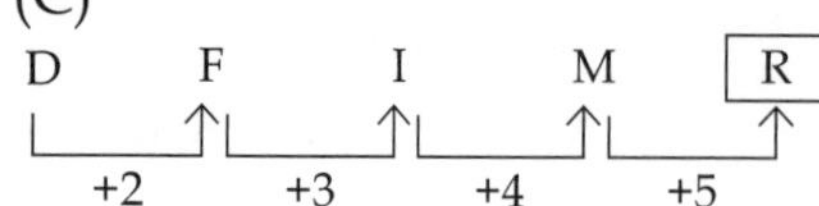

So, the next letter in the series will be R.

2. (B)

It is a combination of 3 series i.e.

P, Q, R, S, ?

Z, Y,X, W, ?

A, C, E G, ?

So,

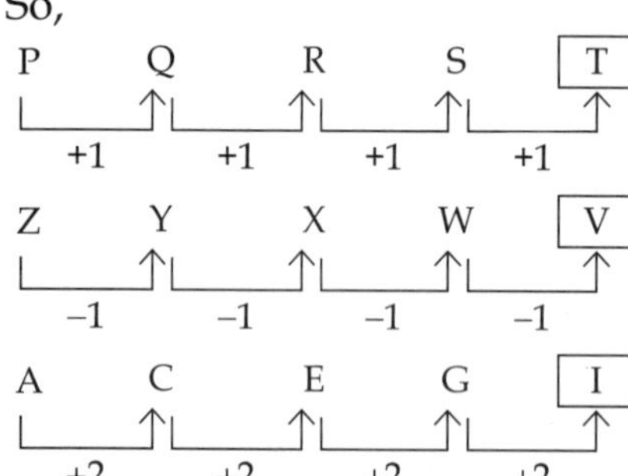

So, the next term will be TVI

3. (A)

It is a combination of 3 series.

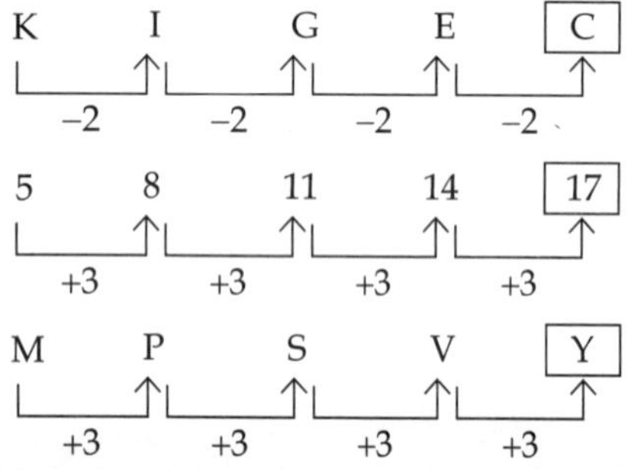

So, the next term will be C17Y.

4. (D)

It is a combination of 3 series.

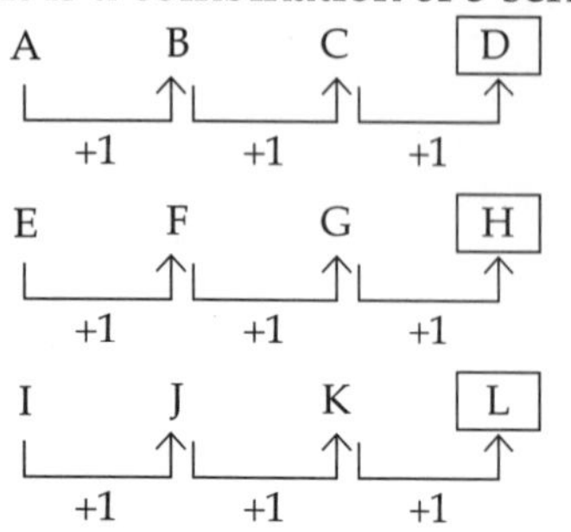

So, the next term will be DHL.

5. (A)

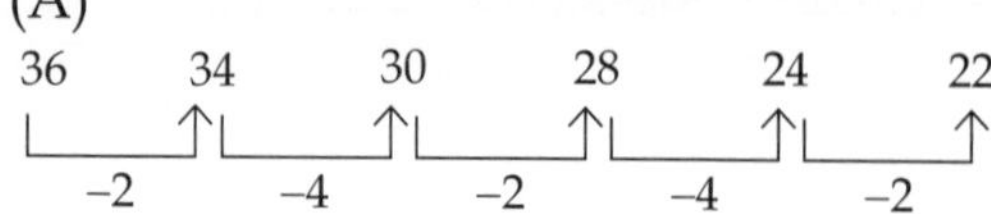

6. (A)

Bullet is used in Gun and in the same way Arrow is used in Bow.

7. (B)

Bald is opposite to Blond. In the same way Barren is opposite to Fertile.

8. (C)

Disease is cured by Medicine. In the same way Famine is controlled by Rainfall.

9. (B)

Socks are made of Nylon and Purse is made of Leather.

10. (D)

Doctor cures the Patient and Lawyer solves the cases of Client.

11. (B)

Except (B), all are items of stationery.

12. (B)

Except (B), all are fruits. Jackfruit is a type of vegetable.

13. (A)

Except (A), all have engines.

14. (A)

Except (A), all are parts of a tree.

15. (C)

Except (C), all are names of birds.

16. (C)

The positions of letters are changed in reverse order.

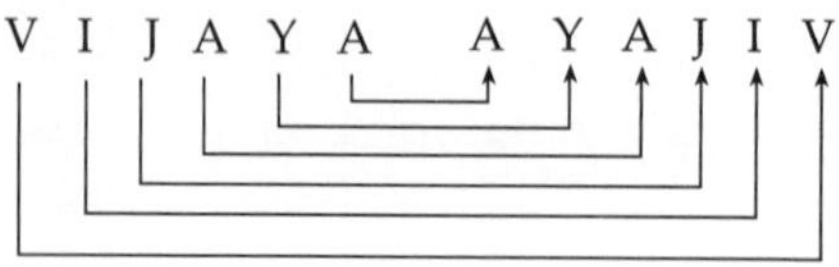

In the same way

17. (B)

R $\xrightarrow{+2}$ T　　　　T $\xrightarrow{+2}$ V

E $\xrightarrow{+2}$ G　Similarly　E $\xrightarrow{+2}$ G

A $\xrightarrow{+2}$ C　　　　A $\xrightarrow{+2}$ C

D $\xrightarrow{+2}$ F　　　　C $\xrightarrow{+2}$ E

So, VGCEJ will be the code of TEACH.

18. (D)

In this question, letters are coded by another letter.

E A R T H　　T E A R

↓ ↓ ↓ ↓ ↓　　↓ ↓ ↓ ↓

S U B D Z　　D S U B

So, DSUB will be the code of TEAR.

19. (D)

Letters are coded by numbers.

B H A S H A　　B R A I N

↓ ↓ ↓ ↓ ↓ ↓ and ↓ ↓ ↓ ↓ ↓

1 5 4 7 5 4　　1 3 4 0 8

Putting the code of A, H, I, N, S and A from above, we get

A H I N S A

↓ ↓ ↓ ↓ ↓ ↓

4 5 0 8 7 4

So, 450874 is the code of AHINSA.

20. (A)

H K U J

−2 −2 −2 −2

↓ ↓ ↓ ↓

F I S H

U V C D

−2 −2 −2 −2

↓ ↓ ↓ ↓

S T A B

So, STAB is the decode (word) of UVCD.

21. (A)

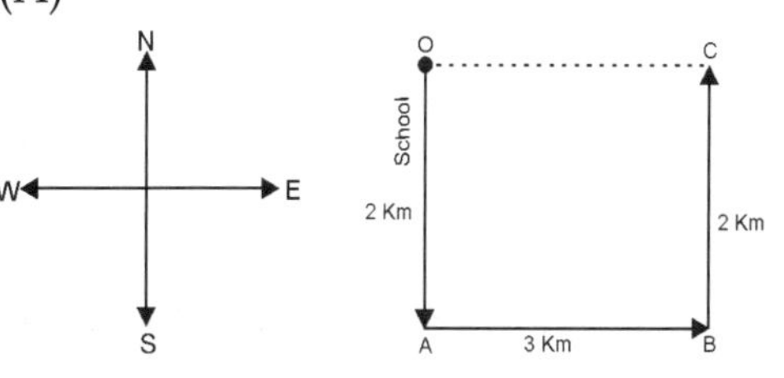

O and C are initial and final positions of Vijay. Clearly, OC = AB = 3 Km.

22. (C)

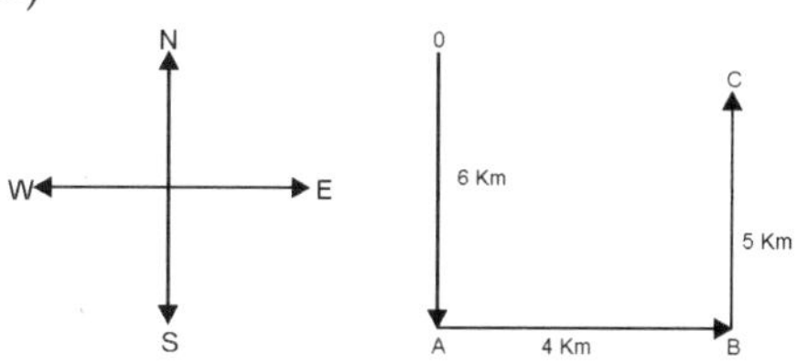

Clearly, Huma's face will be towards North.

23. (B)

As Kailash and Moolchand are in same pair and Kailash's face is towards west, so Moolchand's face will be towards East. Vijay's face is towards North. So, Munesh's face will be towards South. It can be shown like this

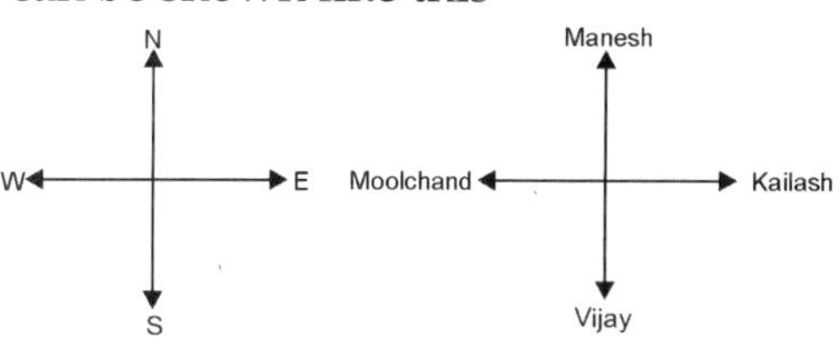

24. (A)

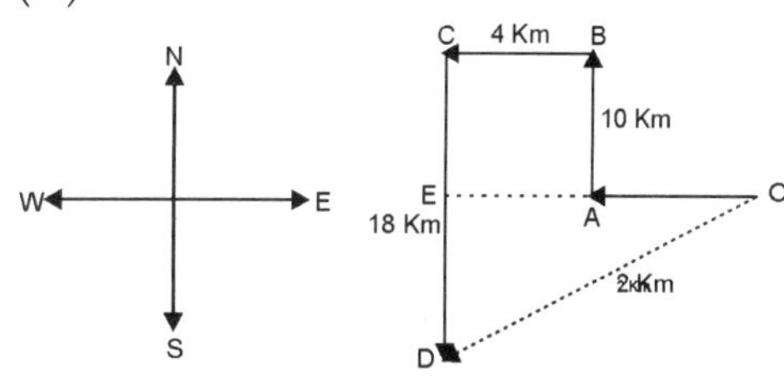

Distance from initial point to final point OD (By Pythagoras theorem)

$$= \sqrt{OE^2 + ED^2}$$

$$= \sqrt{(OA + AE)^2 + ED^2}$$

$$= \sqrt{(OA + BC)^2 + ED^2}$$

$$= \sqrt{(2+4)^2 + 8^2}$$

$$= \sqrt{6^2 + 8^2} = \sqrt{36 + 64}$$

$$= \sqrt{100} = 10$$

25. (C)

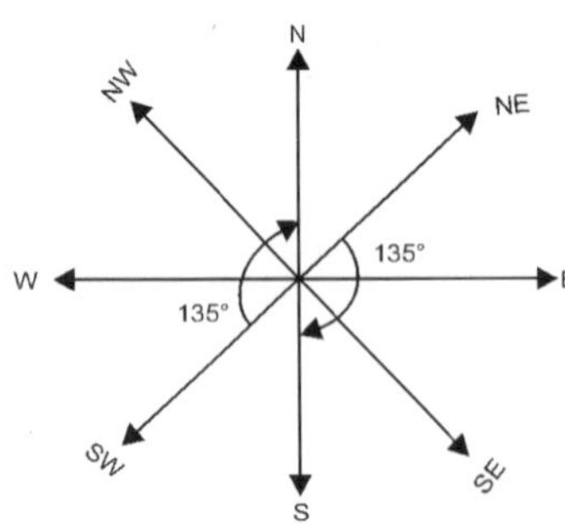

If North-East direction is shifted 135° clockwise, then it becomes South. In the same way, if South-West direction is shifted 135° clockwise, we get North direction.

26. (C)
Jai's position from bottom = Total no. of students – position from top + 1
= 20 – 5 + 1 = 16

10th | Shiv Kumar
20th

27. (A)
No. of students = Shiv Kumar's position from right + his position from Left – 1
= 20 + 10 – 1 = 29

28. (A)
According to question, order of seating arrangement is as follows:
Vijay, Khyati, Sandeep, Rashmi
So, Rashmi is sitting at extreme right.

29. (B)

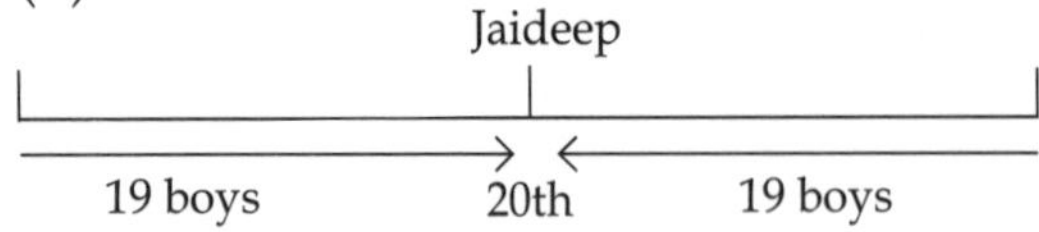

So, total no. of boys = 19 + 19 + 1 = 39

30. (C)
According the question,
Bhiroli > Khanpura,
Jadaul > Bamanpur,
Jugsana > Bhiroli,
Bamanpur > Jugsana
By Combining all these, we get
Jadaul > Bamanpur > Jugsana > Bhiroli > Khanpura
So, Jadaul is the biggest village.

31. (D)
D E B U T
Clearly, DE, BD and UT have as many letters between them as in alphabet.

32. (C)
D O N A T I O N
Clearly, DA, ON and ON have as many letters between them as in alphabet.

33. (B)
The word formed by 2nd, 5th, 9th and 11th letter is 'SOUR.'

34. (C)
Arrangement of words in alphabetical order is Seldom, Selection, Self, Sell, Sender.

35. (A)
Arrangement of words in alphabetical order is Load, Long, Longing, Loose, Lost.

36. (B)
R and S sit opposite to each other. So, if P sits opposite to teacher, Q shall be teacher. Q is to the right of artist. If R is barber, then S on the opposite side shall be doctor or engineer. Thus profession of P is Engineer.

37. (D)
Clearly, from the above explanation, Profession of Q is Teacher.

Sol. (38–40)
Radha < Sulekha < Kanchan < Madhu and Sulekha < Anju < Kanchan
So, Radha < Sulekha < Anju < Kanchan < Madhu.

38. (A)
Kanchan is second tallest.

39. (D)
Kanchan is taller than Anju but shorter than Madhu.

40. (C)
Clearly, Radha is the shortest among all girls.

51. (D)

Figure (X) is embedded in figure (D) as shown below.

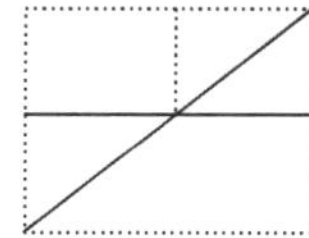

52. (B)

Figure (X) is embedded in figure (B) as shown below.

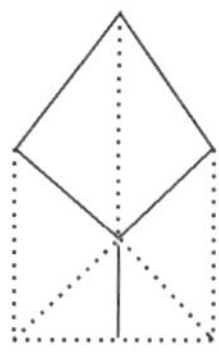

53. (D)

Figure (X) is embedded in figure (D) as shown below.

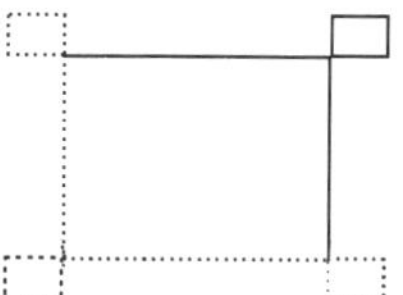

54. (A)

Figure (X) is embedded in figure (A) as shown below.

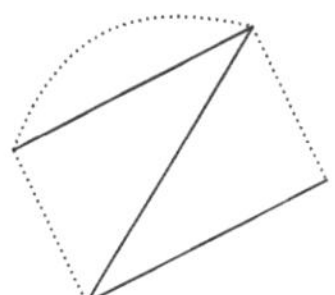

55. (A)

Figure (X) is embedded in figure (A) as shown below.

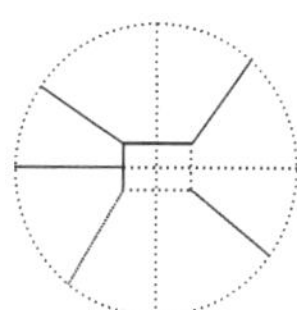

MODEL TEST PAPER

Answer Key

1. (C)	2. (B)	3. (A)	4. (B)	5. (C)	6. (D)	7. (C)	8. (D)	9. (C)	10. (A)
11. (D)	12. (B)	13. (A)	14. (A)	15. (C)	16. (B)	17. (C)	18. (C)	19. (A)	20. (C)
21. (D)	22. (D)	23. (D)	24. (C)	25. (B)	26. (B)	27. (B)	28. (C)	29. (B)	30. (A)
31. (D)	32. (C)	33. (B)	34. (B)	35. (B)	36. (B)	37. (B)	38. (C)	39. (C)	40. (C)
41. (D)	42. (C)	43. (D)	44. (D)	45. (C)	46. (C)	47. (A)	48. (B)	49. (A)	50. (A)

SAMPLE OMR ANSWER SHEET

1. STUDENT NAME (IN ENGLISH CAPITAL LETTERS ONLY)

Students must write and darken the respective circles completely using HB Pencil only. Othewise their Answer Sheets will not be evaluated.

PERSONAL DETAILS

2. SCHOOL CODE

A–Z	A–Z	0–9	0–9	0–9	0–9

3. CLASS

0–1	0–9

4. SECTION

A B C D E F G H I J K L M N O P Q R S T U V W X Y Z

5. ROLL NO.

0–9	0–9	0–9

6. QUESTION PAPER SET

A ○ B ○ C ○ D ○

7. MOBILE NUMBER

Ten columns, each: 0 1 2 4 5 6 7 8 9

8. GENDER

MALE ○

FEMALE ○

9. STREAM (Only for Class XI and XII Students)

MATHEMATICS ○

BIOLOGY ○

OTHERS ○

MARK YOUR ANSWERS

Q.					Q.				
1.	Ⓐ	Ⓑ	Ⓒ	Ⓓ	26.	Ⓐ	Ⓑ	Ⓒ	Ⓓ
2.	Ⓐ	Ⓑ	Ⓒ	Ⓓ	27.	Ⓐ	Ⓑ	Ⓒ	Ⓓ
3.	Ⓐ	Ⓑ	Ⓒ	Ⓓ	28.	Ⓐ	Ⓑ	Ⓒ	Ⓓ
4.	Ⓐ	Ⓑ	Ⓒ	Ⓓ	29.	Ⓐ	Ⓑ	Ⓒ	Ⓓ
5.	Ⓐ	Ⓑ	Ⓒ	Ⓓ	30.	Ⓐ	Ⓑ	Ⓒ	Ⓓ
6.	Ⓐ	Ⓑ	Ⓒ	Ⓓ	31.	Ⓐ	Ⓑ	Ⓒ	Ⓓ
7.	Ⓐ	Ⓑ	Ⓒ	Ⓓ	32.	Ⓐ	Ⓑ	Ⓒ	Ⓓ
8.	Ⓐ	Ⓑ	Ⓒ	Ⓓ	33.	Ⓐ	Ⓑ	Ⓒ	Ⓓ
9.	Ⓐ	Ⓑ	Ⓒ	Ⓓ	34.	Ⓐ	Ⓑ	Ⓒ	Ⓓ
10.	Ⓐ	Ⓑ	Ⓒ	Ⓓ	35.	Ⓐ	Ⓑ	Ⓒ	Ⓓ
11.	Ⓐ	Ⓑ	Ⓒ	Ⓓ	36.	Ⓐ	Ⓑ	Ⓒ	Ⓓ
12.	Ⓐ	Ⓑ	Ⓒ	Ⓓ	37.	Ⓐ	Ⓑ	Ⓒ	Ⓓ
13.	Ⓐ	Ⓑ	Ⓒ	Ⓓ	38.	Ⓐ	Ⓑ	Ⓒ	Ⓓ
14.	Ⓐ	Ⓑ	Ⓒ	Ⓓ	39.	Ⓐ	Ⓑ	Ⓒ	Ⓓ
15.	Ⓐ	Ⓑ	Ⓒ	Ⓓ	40.	Ⓐ	Ⓑ	Ⓒ	Ⓓ
16.	Ⓐ	Ⓑ	Ⓒ	Ⓓ	41.	Ⓐ	Ⓑ	Ⓒ	Ⓓ
17.	Ⓐ	Ⓑ	Ⓒ	Ⓓ	42.	Ⓐ	Ⓑ	Ⓒ	Ⓓ
18.	Ⓐ	Ⓑ	Ⓒ	Ⓓ	43.	Ⓐ	Ⓑ	Ⓒ	Ⓓ
19.	Ⓐ	Ⓑ	Ⓒ	Ⓓ	44.	Ⓐ	Ⓑ	Ⓒ	Ⓓ
20.	Ⓐ	Ⓑ	Ⓒ	Ⓓ	45.	Ⓐ	Ⓑ	Ⓒ	Ⓓ
21.	Ⓐ	Ⓑ	Ⓒ	Ⓓ	46.	Ⓐ	Ⓑ	Ⓒ	Ⓓ
22.	Ⓐ	Ⓑ	Ⓒ	Ⓓ	47.	Ⓐ	Ⓑ	Ⓒ	Ⓓ
23.	Ⓐ	Ⓑ	Ⓒ	Ⓓ	48.	Ⓐ	Ⓑ	Ⓒ	Ⓓ
24.	Ⓐ	Ⓑ	Ⓒ	Ⓓ	49.	Ⓐ	Ⓑ	Ⓒ	Ⓓ
25.	Ⓐ	Ⓑ	Ⓒ	Ⓓ	50.	Ⓐ	Ⓑ	Ⓒ	Ⓓ

Signature of the Student & Date of Examination

Signature of the Invigilator & Date of Examination

V&S Publishers, F-2/16 Ansari Road, Daryaganj, New Delhi-110002, ☎ 011-23240026-27
info@vspublishers.com, www.vspublishers.com